Applying Knowledge Management

Techniques for Building Corporate Memories

Ian Watson
University of Auckland

MORGAN KAUFMANN PUBLISHERS

AN IMPRINT OF ELSEVIER SCIENCE

AMSTERDAM   BOSTON   LONDON   NEW YORK
OXFORD   PARIS   SAN DIEGO   SAN FRANCISCO
SINGAPORE   SYDNEY   TOKYO

Senior Editor	Denise E. M. Penrose
Publishing Services Manager	Edward Wade
Production Editor	Howard Severson
Editorial Coordinator	Emilia Thiuri
Cover Design	Yvo Riezebos
Cover Image	The Image Bank
Text Design	Mark Ong
Illustration	Dartmouth Publishing, Inc.
Composition	Top Graphics
Copyeditor	Judith Brown
Proofreader	Erin Milnes
Indexer	Bill Meyers
Printer	The Maple-Vail Book Manufacturing Group

Designations used by companies to distinguish their products are often claimed as trademarks or registered trademarks. In all instances in which Morgan Kaufmann Publishers is aware of a claim, the product names appear in initial capital or all capital letters. Readers, however, should contact the appropriate companies for more complete information regarding trademarks and registration.

Morgan Kaufmann Publishers
An imprint of Elsevier Science
340 Pine Street, Sixth Floor
San Francisco, CA 94104-3205
www.mkp.com

06 05 04 03 02   5 4 3 2 1

Library of Congress Control Number: 2002108512
ISBN: 1-55860-760-9

This book is printed on acid-free paper.

For KB

Contents

Part II Case Studies 47

Chapter 3 Managing Product Quality: Total Recall at National Semiconductor 49

Chapter 4   Developing Expertise: Color Matching at General Electric Plastics   87

Chapter 7   Information Retrieval: Intelligent Online Product Selection for Analog Devices   163

Chapter 8   Distributed Sales Support: Web-Based Engineering at Western Air   179

Chapter 9   Personalizing Information Services: Intelligent Digital TV at ChangingWorlds   201

Part III   Conclusion   215

Chapter 10   Lessons Learned   217

Preface

In 1997 I published a book that introduced case-based reasoning (CBR) to a less specialized audience than the one usually targeted by CBR publications. My book was intended as an introductory text for students, general software and programming professionals, MIS managers, and those responsible for corporate IT thinking and implementation. The book was a success, and I received many emails from readers saying how helpful they found it. However, writing any book is a compromise. I wanted to introduce the concepts behind CBR, describe ways it was applied, and illustrate how CBR tools could be used to develop successful applications. What I was not able to do was to describe case studies of successful commercially fielded applications in sufficient detail to give confidence to a corporate developer looking to implement a CBR system.

So in the summer of 1999 I approached Denise Penrose, my editor at Morgan Kaufmann, with the idea of publishing a collection of case studies of CBR applications and was told to develop the idea. Over the years I had become aware of many interesting uses of CBR, and I decided that a book would have greater veracity if the developers of the systems described their applications in their own words. I would write a couple of introductory chapters, providing readers who were new to the field with the background knowledge required to understand the case studies, and then write a concluding chapter highlighting the lessons learned from the case studies.

In 2000 I started to collect case studies and, somewhat disruptively, moved from England to New Zealand. Over the next couple of years, case studies were collated and edited, the dotcom bubble burst, some companies disappeared, and others were taken over. As a consequence of all this "restructuring," some case studies were dropped, and others were extended as the success of their deployment grew.

In parallel to this, another change took place. CBR had grown out of artificial intelligence research, namely, machine learning and expert systems. Increasingly, however, conferences were placing CBR applications in knowledge management sessions, and CBR papers were appearing in knowledge management journals. It was around this time that I realized that CBR was not a specific technology, like neural networks or rule-based systems, but was actually a methodology for problem solving.[1] Then at a workshop I helped organize on artificial intelligence and knowledge management, I realized that, not only was CBR a methodology for problem solving, but it was also uniquely matched to the specific processes that a knowledge management system required.[2] Thus, the focus of this book changed during its writing, from being a book intended to showcase successful applications of CBR to one that would demonstrate that CBR could be successfully applied to knowledge management problems.

The book is divided into three parts. In Part One the first chapter introduces you to the background and motivation behind knowledge management (KM) and outlines the main activities or processes in a KM system. I must be explicit here: this book does not deal with KM from the usual management perspective of the majority of KM books. That is, the book does not concern itself with how a knowledge-sharing

---

1 Watson, I. (1999). "CBR Is a Methodology Not a Technology." In *Knowledge Based Systems Journal*, Vol. 12. no. 5-6, Oct. 1999, pp. 303–8. Elsevier, UK.
2 Watson, I. (2000). "Report on Expert Systems 99 Workshop: Using AI to Enable Knowledge Management." In *Expert Update*, Vol. 3 No. 2, pp. 36–38.

culture can be created within an organization. I do not underestimate the importance of this, but it has been well covered in many other places.

The second chapter describes CBR in a sufficient level of detail to help readers new to CBR and knowledge management to understand the case studies. If you need more information on the specifics of CBR implementations, software, and tools, the chapter provides pointers for further reading. The purpose of this chapter is to show how the processes of CBR match the requirements of a KM system.

Part Two comprises seven chapters, each describing a case study of a knowledge management system using CBR. The case studies were chosen to reflect a variety of organizations, business sectors, and applications. All are commercially deployed; they are not research prototypes.

One class of CBR systems has not been showcased here, namely, help desk systems. This is because, again, these systems are well described in other places. Although CBR is ideally suited to support help desks and customer service centers, the special requirements of call-tracking and customer relationship management systems might obscure the knowledge management benefits this book highlights. However, it is worth noting that the companies listed in the Appendix all do the majority of their work in customer relationship management, and moreover, CBR's first major commercial successes were and remain in help desk applications.

Part Three consists of the final chapter, which uses a simple technique to highlight lessons learned from the preceding case studies. From your own organizational context you may well be able to draw out other lessons. I am obviously limited by my own background and context. The book ends with an Appendix that lists CBR software vendors and consultants.

There are many other people who I have to thank for helping me, either directly or indirectly. First, I thank Denise Penrose at Morgan Kaufmann for supporting the project and being so patient with the delays caused by my relocating to the other side of the planet. Obviously I'm indebted to the authors of the case studies, without which the book would not have happened. I'm also grateful to the reviewers of the early drafts who made many sensible suggestions, and in particular to Rick Magaldi of British Airways, who provided such constructive criticism. I hope the reviewers will see that I have made many of the changes suggested, but will recognize that sometimes they had contradictory views. However, this book would have been worse without their input.

I would not have had the time to write this book if it were not for support from the University of Auckland and its computer science department. They have provided me with the time to work on this project and not complained about the numerous "working @ home" emails I sent in. Moreover, they funded my trips to overseas meetings, helping me to establish and maintain the network of contacts without which I could not have obtained the case studies. Thanks are therefore due in particular to my HoD, John Hosking.

No book comes to print without many people being involved in the publication process. Once again, the entire team at Morgan Kaufmann has been totally helpful at all stages, in particular Denise Penrose, Emilia Thiuri, and Howard Severson.

Finally, I would like to thank New Zealand for being the most perfect country in the world and Karen for helping me enjoy the time I wasn't working.

Ian Watson,
August 2002,
Auckland, New Zealand.

I

Corporate Memory

1

Knowledge Management and Organizational Memory

1.1 Introduction

The function of knowledge management is to allow an organization to leverage its information resources and knowledge assets by remembering and applying experience. Knowledge, and consequently its management, is currently being touted as the basis of future economic competitiveness, for example:

> In the information age knowledge, rather than physical assets or resources is the key to competitiveness. What is new about attitudes to knowledge today is the recognition of the need to harness, manage and use it like any other asset. This raises issues not only of appropriate processes and systems, but also how to account for knowledge in the balance sheet.[1]

Entrepreneurs are no longer seen as the owners of capital, but rather as individuals who know how to do things. The introduction of information technology on a wide scale in the last thirty years has made the

---

1 Moran, N. Becoming a Knowledge Based Organization, Financial Times Survey. *Knowledge Management*, 28 April 1999, London, UK.

capturing and distribution of knowledge widespread, and brought to the forefront the issue of the management of knowledge assets. Thus, *knowledge management* is spreading throughout organizations, from information management systems to marketing and human resources.

With knowledge now being viewed as a significant asset, the creation and sharing of knowledge has become an important factor within and between organizations. However, many writers refer to the "paradox of value" when considering the nature of knowledge, in particular its intangibility and inappropriateness as an asset and the difficulty of assessing and protecting its value.

This chapter introduces you to the basics of knowledge management, to help you understand what knowledge is, to show you that knowledge has a life cycle, and to explain the importance of managing it. The chapter concludes by introducing you to the case-based reasoning cycle, showing how it matches the requirements of the knowledge management life cycle. Chapter 2 then describes in greater detail how case-based reasoning works.

1.2   A Definition of Knowledge Management

Books on technical subjects often start with definitions, but defining knowledge management is not easy. Different writers approach the subject from different perspectives and with different motives. They therefore have different definitions. Most knowledge management literature treats *knowledge* broadly, and uses it to cover all that an organization needs to know to perform its functions. This may involve formalized knowledge, patents, laws, programs, and procedures, as well as the more intangible know-how, skills, and experience of people. It can also include the way that organizations function, communicate, analyze situations, develop new solutions to problems, and develop new ways of doing business. Moreover, it may involve issues of culture, custom, and values as well as relationships with suppliers and customers.

Management includes all the ways in which an organization's knowledge assets are handled, including how knowledge is gathered, stored, transmitted, applied, updated, or generated. However, the majority of texts on knowledge management focus more strongly on the management of the organization as a whole, to create an environment where knowledge management can succeed. I do not underestimate the importance of creating a whole management ethos that is supportive of knowledge management, but I believe that these issues have been well covered by many other writers. Consequently, this book focuses on the management of the knowledge itself, through the application of a single methodology for implementing knowledge management solutions, namely, case-based reasoning (CBR).

Thus, a working definition of knowledge management for this book is:

Knowledge management involves the acquisition, storage, retrieval, application, generation, and review of the knowledge assets of an organization in a controlled way.

As this book develops, you will see how this pragmatic definition is appropriate to the knowledge management methodology (that is, CBR) used by the case studies.

1.3   Why Manage Knowledge?

Knowledge has always been valuable to people. Great cultures and civilizations are often remembered or distinguished by their libraries: the great library of Alexandria of antiquity, the British Library, or the Library of Congress all house the knowledge of a civilization. Thus, in a sense, knowledge management has always been around us; yet it was not until recently that the term was widely used.[2]

---

2 I am not going to make myself a hostage to eager researchers by attempting to give a precise date for the coinage of the term *knowledge management.*

Many of us are now familiar with phrases like *knowledge economy* and *knowledge workers.* Whereas the key to wealth creation was once ownership or access to capital or natural resources, this has now been joined by access to or the creation of knowledge. Thus, college kids with smart new ideas can generate billions of dollars. This statement does not refer to recent dotcom startups, but to well-established, highly profitable companies like Microsoft, Cisco Systems, Oracle, and Sun— all of which were started from scratch by college kids with nothing but knowledge, passion, and vision.

Where once it was usual to fell trees, mine gold, or forge steel to create wealth, now whole sectors rely on servicing each others' needs to create wealth. Indeed, many argue it has always been so, since it was not the forty-niners but rather those who sold the miners shovels and whiskey who made the real fortunes.

Many major corporations now realize that they are successful because of the skills and experience of their employees, not because of some physical asset they control. Moreover, even if they have cornered the global market in some commodity, times change and people's needs alter.

There has also been another great change in the last decades. Most of us no longer expect to work for the same company all our lives. The idea of a "company man," who works for the same organization from the time he leaves school to retirement, is seen as almost a Victorian idea. Reengineering, down-sizing, right-sizing, out-sourcing, all have created an employment market that is much more fluid, with skilled employees moving between projects and companies. A consequence of this is that many companies that reengineered in the 1990s discovered that they had lost valuable skills and experience. Thus, partly through the problems created by successive management revolutions, companies recognized that their knowledge of what and how they did things was a key asset that needed to be explicitly managed, just as they would manage other valuable corporate assets.

1.4 What Is Knowledge?

In order to manage something you must be able to recognize it. Knowledge does not exist in isolation though. It is not something that can be picked up or locked in a company vault. Indeed, some philosophers believe that knowledge is a human construct that cannot exist outside the mind of a person. It is worth considering the relationship between knowledge and concepts like data and information. Computers have been managing data (as in database management systems) for decades. You are also probably familiar with the term *information systems* and perhaps have even heard of knowledge-based systems.

Data, information, and knowledge can be considered, not as discrete entities, but as existing along a continuum, as illustrated in Figure 1.1. They exhibit a relationship with their context and the amount of understanding they either impart or require.

For example, data that is independent of any context—the number 9 perhaps—does not require any understanding or provide any. If that data item is placed in a context, such as "street number = 9," we have some understanding that there is a relationship between "street number" and "9." Most of us know that house numbers usually increment in even numbers on one side of the street and odd numbers on the

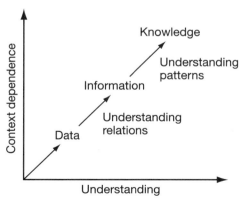

Figure 1.1 The relationship of context to understanding.

other side. This knowledge would lead us to expect to find houses number 7 and 11 on either side of house number 9. Knowledge might also tell us that street numbers often increase as we travel away from the town or city center. Thus, we could infer that house number 9 is closer to the town center than house number 101.

An important notion here is that knowledge involves the recognition or the understanding of patterns. This involves the creation of mental models, exemplars, or archetypes. We may all have a mental model of a town that has a central square or intersection where First Avenue is bisected by First or Main Street. This archetype (or knowledge) can be used to help us navigate in unfamiliar towns.[3]

When a pattern exists amidst the information, the pattern has the potential to represent knowledge. However, the patterns representing knowledge must have a context. The context of the pattern provides a degree of predictability as to when the pattern is applicable. This notion of the reliability or applicability of a pattern is an important concept that we will return to in the following chapter.

Most of us have a casual familiarity with knowledge: we think we can recognize knowledge when we come across it. For instance, we know that a work colleague or a friend is *knowledgeable* about a certain subject. You may feel that you are knowledgeable about many subjects, such as debugging Windows NT systems, baking bread, or playing Jamaican reggae music. But this casual familiarity hides deeper complexity. The sort of knowledge you can easily recognize is *explicit* knowledge—explicit in the sense that it can be codified or written down. Thus, you can go to a bookstore and buy books on Windows NT, baking, and reggae music. You can even study and sit exams in some of these subjects.

However, not all knowledge is explicit; some is tacit. It can be felt and understood but not expressed. You can buy a cookbook to show

---

3 Anyone who has lived or traveled in the Old World knows that this archetype is practically useless in, for example, a southern Italian town because the context is different.

you how to bake bread, and it can give you recipes, ingredients, quantities, and techniques; but no book can really tell you what the bread dough should feel like when it has been properly kneaded. Instead, books will say something like "knead the dough for five minutes or until elastic." A much better solution is to have an experienced baker show you what bread dough feels like when it has been properly kneaded. After time you will acquire the tacit knowledge of how bread dough should feel, but you in turn would not be able to tell anyone how it feels directly and would have to use similes like "warm chewing gum."

Early expert or knowledge-based systems codified and operationalized explicit knowledge. But knowledge management systems must deal with both explicit and tacit knowledge. To many people in the knowledge management community, it is wrong to attempt to codify (that is, to make explicit) all knowledge, and attempts to do so result in much tacit knowledge being lost.

Thus, the knowledge representations used by a knowledge management system must be flexible. The rigid formalisms of rule-based expert systems from the 1980s are too restrictive to handle tacit knowledge. The more discursive representation of a library of case histories, such as those employed by case-based reasoning systems, may be better able to deal with tacit knowledge; although you should recognize that no formalization exists that can adequately capture all tacit knowledge.

If you like simple experiments, try to write down a method for reliably bouncing a ball off a wall and catching it. You could use geometry and physics to describe the arc that the ball travels and to predict its rebound, but I doubt that you make those calculations in your head when you actually catch a ball. Without using formal methods, you are left with statements like "keep your eye on the ball," which does not actually say much about the process of catching. Catching a ball requires tacit knowledge that most of us acquire as a child through hours of practice. It becomes a reflex and something that is very hard to articulate. Such knowledge is almost impossible to make explicit and codify. However, from an organization's point of view—for example, a baseball team—it is useful to make explicit the knowledge of who on the team is a particularly good catcher. Managing such knowledge would be useful to them. Hence, knowledge management often encompasses "who knows what" as well as "what is known."

This brings us to the notion of experience as storytelling. A story told within a social context is one method that can be used to transfer knowledge. The importance of context in making knowledge explicit should not be underestimated. Stories are rich constructs used to convey personal experience. Drama, humor, repetition, caricature, and exaggeration are devices used to convey important principles, details, or experience to people. A storytelling approach and the interaction with peers in a social context can be a prerequisite to efficient generalization from experience. This is one reason why the debriefing is such an important part of military operations: This is what we planned. This is what we did. This was the outcome. How did we do against expectations? Have we learned anything new? What would we do differently in future?

You will see in subsequent case studies that it is the contextualization of experience that often makes a case-based reasoner effective. Stories can act as a bridge between the hidden inner mental world and the explicit formalized world. Remembering often seems to be enhanced by the use of metaphor and social context. The oral tradition of the remembering and telling of stories was once a vital way of preserving cultural community in preliterate societies. Shamans, bards, priests, and other storytellers were consequently people of special status within such societies. Thus we can deduce that knowledge management as a concept has a lineage going back to the dawn of human society.

1.5 What Knowledge Should I Be Managing?

What knowledge should I be managing? This question might seem trivial, but in fact it is quite hard to answer. A trite answer is, "Everything!" But of course if you attempted to capture and collate everything, you would be swamped, information overload would soon set in, and you would not be able to distinguish high-value, reliable, and useful information and knowledge from low-value, dubious knowledge.

The knowledge that you need to manage is that which is critical to your company—that which adds value to your products or to your services. Here are some examples:

- Knowledge of a particular job, such as how to fix a fault in a piece of critical manufacturing equipment.
- Knowledge of who knows what in a company, who solved a similar problem last time.
- Knowledge of who is best to perform a particular job or task, who has the latest training or best qualifications in a particular subject.
- Knowledge of corporate history—has this process been tried before, what was the outcome?
- Knowledge of a particular customer account and knowledge of similar customers.
- Knowledge of how to put together a team that can work on a project, who has worked successfully together in the past, what skills were needed on similar projects.

To this list I'm sure you can add knowledge from your own company or organization that should be managed. It is worth noting, however, that knowledge management systems need not attempt to manage all the knowledge in a company. That may well be the long-term goal, but most knowledge management projects start out with much more modest ambitions and concentrate on the management of a single knowledge area or domain.

1.6   Toward a Knowledge Framework

A common approach to considering knowledge emphasizes its relationship to information in terms of difference. This perceived distinction between information and knowledge is not helpful and has

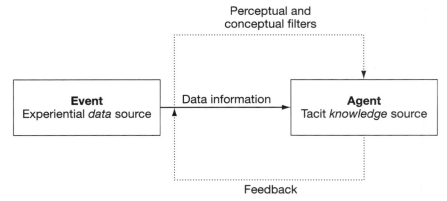

Figure 1.2   Data, information, and knowledge (after Boisot).[5]

led to the current confused preoccupation in the management literature with what is conceived of as a clear distinction between "knowledge management" and "information management." Information and
knowledge are more appropriately seen in terms of a dynamic and interactive relationship. Information facilitates the development of
knowledge, which creates more information that deepens knowledge,
ad infinitum. For example, Nonaka and Takeuchi stated:

> Information provides a new point of view for interpreting events or ob-
> jects, which makes visible previously invisible meanings or sheds light on
> unexpected connections. Thus, information is a necessary medium or ma-
> terial for eliciting and constructing knowledge[4].

The dynamic nature of this relationship is illustrated in Figure 1.2.
Looking at information purely in terms of the degree to which it
has been processed—that is, the data, information, knowledge contin-

---

4 Nonaka, I. and Takeuchi, H. (1995). *The Knowledge-Creating Company: How
   Japanese Companies Create the Dynamics of Innovation,* Oxford University Press.

5 Boisot, M. (1998). *Knowledge Assets: Securing Competitive Advantage in the
   Information Economy,* Oxford University Press.

uum—oversimplifies the complex relationship between the three intangibles. Stewart, a knowledge management guru, notes:

> The idea that knowledge can be slotted into a data-wisdom hierarchy is bogus, for the simple reason that one man's knowledge is another man's data.[6]

Note the feedback element within Figure 1.2, which illustrates the dynamic and interactive relationship of information and knowledge as a positive feedback loop.

Data is discrimination between states—for example, black, white, heavy, light, dark—that may or may not convey information to a person, depending on the person's prior stock of knowledge and the context. For example, the states of nature indicated by red, amber, and green traffic lights may not be seen as informative to Bushmen of the Kalahari. Yet they in turn may perceive certain patterns in the soil as indicative of the presence of lions nearby. These patterns would probably convey no knowledge to a New Yorker. (See Figure 1.3.)

Thus, we can characterize data as a property of things and knowledge as a property of people, which predisposes them to act in particular circumstances. Information is that subset of the data residing in things that causes a person to act; it is filtered from the data by the person's perceptual or conceptual apparatus.

1.7   Knowledge Management Activities

As I have said, this book will not discuss the cultural and organizational activities that are well covered in other texts on knowledge management. Disregarding these—though I accept their crucial importance—the act of managing knowledge (rather than managing the

---

6   Stewart, T.A. (1997). *Intellectual Capital,* Nicholas Brealey, London.

Figure 1.3   Deriving knowledge from patterns is contextual.

people that manage knowledge) can be characterized by the following four activities:

1. acquire knowledge (learn, create, or identify);
2. analyze knowledge (assess, validate, or value);
3. preserve knowledge (organize, represent, or maintain); and
4. use knowledge (apply, transfer, or share).

Don't get too concerned by the choice of words used here, but accept that to manage knowledge you must first have some knowledge to manage, you may need to analyze the knowledge you have, you will need to store the knowledge, and of course you will want to be able to access and use the knowledge in the future.

These activities do not exist in isolation. Instead, you can think of them as a cycle, as shown in Figure 1.4. You can view this knowledge

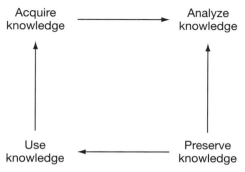

Figure 1.4   The KM-cycle

management cycle (the KM-cycle) as a simplification of the more detailed CBR-cycle discussed shortly. The element that links the cycle is the use of knowledge, since it is likely that when knowledge is used, a new insight into the knowledge may be created. This new knowledge must in turn be acquired, analyzed, and preserved for future use.

Knowledge management is a continuing cyclical process with no end, not a linear one with a single goal. A knowledge management system will therefore be continually evolving, or learning, and any technology used to implement it must support evolution and learning. This point is worth repeating: knowledge management is a continuous ongoing process, not something you do once.

The next section will show you conceptually how case-based reasoning provides mechanisms for dealing with each of these four core knowledge management activities and how it maps to the KM-cycle.

1.8   A Methodology for Knowledge Management

At a recent workshop held at Cambridge University in England, a group of people active in knowledge management and artificial intelligence identified the main activities needed by a knowledge management system.[7] These were mapped to artificial intelligence methods or techniques. The main knowledge management activities were identified as the acquisition, analysis, preservation, and use of knowledge. This section will show how case-based reasoning can meet each of these requirements.

Case-based reasoning is a methodology for supporting knowledge management. It is not important now that you know what CBR is or how it works; this will be explained in the next chapter. For now just consider the classic definition of CBR:

> A case-based reasoner solves problems by using or adapting solutions to old problems.[8]

This definition tells us what a case-based reasoner does, not how it does what it does. It is a methodology.[9] The set of CBR principles are more fully defined as a cycle comprising six activities or processes, called the CBR-cycle, as shown in Figure 1.5. The six activities (called the six-REs by the CBR Community) are as follows:

1. Retrieve knowledge that matches the knowledge requirement.
2. Reuse a selection of the knowledge retrieved.
3. Revise or adapt that knowledge in light of its use if necessary.
4. Review the new knowledge to see if it is worth retaining.
5. Retain the new knowledge if indicated by step 4.
6. Refine the knowledge in the knowledge memory as necessary.

The six-REs of the CBR-cycle can be mapped directly to the activities required by a KM-cycle shown in Figure 1.4, as follows:

---

7 Watson, I. (2000). "Report on Expert Systems 99 Workshop: Using AI to Enable Knowledge Management." In *Expert Update*, Vol. 3 No. 2, pp. 36–38. ISSN 1465-4091.

8 Riebeck, C.K., & Schank, R. (1989). *Inside Case-Based Reasoning.* Erlbaum, Northvale, NJ.

9 A methodology may be defined as *"an organised set of principles which guide action in trying to 'manage' (in the broad sense) real-world problem situations."* Checkland, P. and Scholes, J. (1990). *Soft Systems Methodology in Action,* Wiley, New York.

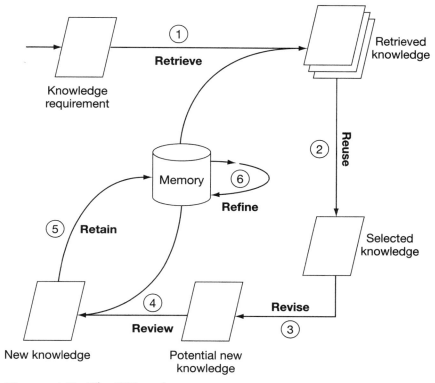

Figure 1.5 The CBR-cycle.

1. The processes of retrieval, reuse, and revision support the acquisition of knowledge.
2. The processes of review and refinement support the analysis of knowledge.
3. The memory itself (along with retrieval and refinement) supports the preservation of knowledge.
4. Finally, retrieval, reuse, and revision support the use of knowledge.

It's OK if you do not understand how these processes work now. The next chapter will explain the CBR-cycle in more detail, and then these processes will be illustrated by the case studies.

1.9 Vignette: Managing Knowledge at Microsoft

To contextualize your understanding of knowledge management, we will end with a brief case study. In the age of e-commerce, few brands have a more commanding presence than Microsoft. For millions of people and hundreds of thousands of companies around the globe, Microsoft operating systems and software applications are indispensable components of their work and home environments. But that extraordinary presence comes with an equally compelling challenge. As a direct consequence of the company's scope and market penetration, Microsoft must grapple with one of the industry's most daunting customer service loads. This vignette dramatically shows the benefits of knowledge management using an organizational memory.

> "Last year our customer satisfaction data identified two areas for improvement in the customer care arena," noted Helen Pickup, Director of Microsoft's Customer Care Centre in Glasgow, Scotland. "Customers were finding it difficult to contact us and, once contact was made, the experience was inconsistent. In order to address this we put together a strategy that focused on both access and service."

Microsoft's strategy encompassed two important tactical moves. First, the company's three major contact points were consolidated into a single channel for all customers. Second, customer service representatives were trained as "knowledge brokers," tasked with handling inquiries across all products, programs, and services, rather than relying on a procedure that routed the customer to an appropriate specialist. "The overall goal," according to Pickup, "was to drive up first contact resolution and improve the customer experience."

"From the outset," Pickup continued, "it was clear that this strategy relied on us being able to implement a knowledge management system that would put all the information on our products, programs, and services at the agents' fingertips." After reviewing a number of technologies, Microsoft engaged Project Techniques, a consulting firm, to help evaluate and identify the best solution. Microsoft's call center outsourcer, Thus PLC, also participated in the evaluation process.

The first step in the process was to identify the type of organizational memory that would satisfy Microsoft's requirements. Project Techniques reviewed the relative merits of each of the main knowledge management technologies: knowledge-based systems, natural language search, and case-based reasoning (CBR). The goal was to find a tool that would provide both technical and nontechnical agents with easy, structured access to the knowledge base. This led them to select CBR over the other available technologies.

Following an extensive evaluation of CBR applications, Microsoft chose eGain's CBR product, which captures the full range of customer service, sales, and support data in a single organizational memory and deploys that information across the entire contact center.[10] Furthermore, support agents can use different levels of the product based on factors such as user expertise, the customer's situation, or the communication medium (for example, online customer self-service, live Web collaboration, and email).

One of the most important advantages offered by CBR technology lies in its natural, conversational interface. Support agents are provided with information structured to mimic the way people think and speak. Other information retrieval applications, such as keyword search systems, typically are not equipped with sophisticated search refinement capabilities. As a result, keywords often return too many hits, and misspelled or incorrect keywords return none. With CBR, when the agent fails to find a solution on the first attempt, the application will ask a further question designed to refine the search, similar to the way people engage in conversation.

Once the application was deployed in the call center, Microsoft managers discovered another important by-product of CBR technology, namely, its user-friendliness. "The implementation allowed us to place the information that was needed to handle a wide variety of calls

---

10 Contact details for CBR tool vendors can be found in the appendix.

at the agents' fingertips," stated Thus PLC's operations manager. "This reduced our reliance on training and accelerated the speed at which our agents were able to get up and running in the new model."

Within nine months following the implementation of a CBR knowledge management system, Microsoft reported:

- a 10 percent improvement in overall customer satisfaction rating;
- a 28 percent increase in "first-time-fix" success rate;
- a 13 percent increase in the "agent is informed" customer survey score;
- a significant reduction in the time required to train new agents, as well as to elevate existing agent skill sets to the expert level;
- a much wider range of customer care issues handled by individual agents, who also delivered more consistent responses, regardless of the problem.

Summarizing Microsoft's venture into knowledge management, Helen Pickup declared, "We are confident that knowledge management is key to success in the customer care arena. We expect to continue investment in this area."

1.10 Conclusion

This chapter has introduced you to knowledge management. A bibliography of knowledge management literature is included at the end of this book if you would like to read more on this subject. You should understand that knowledge is worth managing: it is valuable to organizations, and it should be treated as a corporate asset. However, knowledge is not always tangible like a patent or other intellectual property; much of it is difficult, perhaps impossible to codify.

The key points you should take away from this chapter are that:

- Knowledge is not static; it evolves. Any knowledge management system must be able to support the acquisition, analysis, preservation, and reuse of knowledge as a continual cyclical process.

■ Knowledge exists in two forms: explicit knowledge that can be codified and tacit knowledge that cannot always be codified. If a knowledge representation is too formalized, much tacit knowledge will be lost. Thus knowledge representations for knowledge management systems must be flexible and discursive.

The next chapter will explain what case-based reasoning is and reinforce its suitability for knowledge management.

2

Understanding Case-Based Reasoning

2.1 Introduction

Chapter 1 introduced the CBR-cycle and showed how it satisfied the requirements of a knowledge management system. In this chapter, we are going to look at each process of the CBR-cycle in more detail. We are also going to look at ways of thinking about or conceptualizing CBR and define terms so you can understand the case studies that follow. This chapter also discusses some of the assumptions that underlie CBR—things that must be true in the world for your use of CBR to be appropriate.

You are going to read the following words often during this book: *similarity* and *retrieval*. If you are a newcomer to CBR, you will learn that CBR uses the concept of similarity to retrieve things (cases) from a library (a case base). Cases are used in many situations; for example, to provide product information to a client, solve a problem in a customer support center, configure manufacturing equipment, or solve complex financial problems.

If you are looking for a detailed formal description of CBR, perhaps involving math or logic, you have picked up the wrong book. If, however, after reading this chapter you think, "CBR seems pretty straightforward," then I have done my job.

CBR is simple. This contributes to its success, as you will see repeatedly in the case study chapters.

2.2 What Is CBR?

Remember when you first visited a strange town or city, perhaps to visit friends. The first time you made that trip, what did you do? Well, I'm going to assume that since you are reading this book you are an organized sort of person. So, you probably consulted a map and planned your route. You worked out whether you should drive or perhaps take a plane and a taxi. If you decided to drive, you noted the highway numbers and intersections, and perhaps the people you were going to visit gave you directions into the city. "Take the 101 and take the first exit past the football stadium, then turn right at the gas station and go three blocks, then left at the burger stand. We are 100 yards down on the right, by the big elm tree. There's usually a red Miata parked outside."

What did you do the next time you visited the same people, and the next? My bet is that once you have been to a place a couple of times you no longer need to plan your trip because you can remember the route. Now suppose the people you visit move a couple of blocks away from their old address. They are now in a new location, a place you have never been before. However, you do not need to plan your next trip from scratch. You can reuse all your old knowledge and just figure out how to go from where your friends used to live to their new address. This might not be the most efficient route—you may drive a few extra blocks—but you will get there just fine.

That process of remembering an old plan, reusing it, and perhaps adapting a small part of it is CBR. We do it all the time, and now computers do it too.

2.3 Case-Based Reasoners Remember

If you drive a car, particularly an older model, after a short time you become familiar with its little quirks and you learn what to do about them. That is case-based reasoning. If you are a parent, remember the responsibility you felt when you brought your first child home. So much was new and strange, because despite all the books you read on parenting, you had no experience. Grandparents are so appreciated then because they remember many of the common problems and know how to solve them.

So you see, CBR is ubiquitous among people, but it has only been recently that computers have been able to use experience and, above all, learn from new experiences.

2.4 The CBR-Cycle

Let's consider a concrete (though greatly simplified) situation. Assume you work for a bank and have to advise on the suitability of a person for a loan. As a banker, you do not want to lend money to people who will be unable to repay the loan. However, your caution must be balanced against a desire not to turn people down needlessly. After all, the bank makes a profit from the interest people pay on loans.

One way of solving your problem is to compare each new loan enquiry against your knowledge of loans you have granted in the past. Let's also assume you have worked for the bank for many years and have an exceptionally good memory! If a person's circumstances are similar to someone who successfully repaid a loan in the past, then you would grant the loan. Conversely, if his or her circumstances are similar to someone who defaulted on a loan, then you wouldn't grant the loan.

Let us examine what tasks you are performing mentally in solving this problem:

- You are searching your memory of previous loans and making an assessment of similarity.
- You attempt to infer an answer from the similar loans you remember.
- You may have to make allowances and adjustments for changes in circumstances over the years; for example, $20,000 is a small salary in 2002 but may not have been such a small salary twenty years ago.
- If you grant the loan, you will monitor and record the outcome of the loan for future use, revising and altering your judgment on what constitutes a good or bad loan as necessary.

You have just mentally gone through the processes of the CBR-cycle.

It is clear from thinking about how we solve many problems that we use our experience and that we are able to learn from new experiences. Let's formalize that process. CBR was described by six activities occurring in a cycle, as discussed in the previous chapter.

This cycle is made up of six processes:

1. Retrieve
2. Reuse
3. Revise
4. Review
5. Retain
6. Refine

Each of these will be described in turn, but first you need to understand what it is that is being retrieved, reused, revised, and so on—namely, cases.

2.5 Cases

Cases are records of experiences that contain knowledge, which can be both explicit and tacit. For example, they can be cases in the legal sense, they can be case histories of patients in the medical sense, details of bank loans, or descriptions of equipment troubleshooting situations. Perhaps you see a pattern emerging. Each of these—a legal case, a medical case history, a bank loan—and the troubleshooting record comprise:

- a *description* (the legal problem, the patient's symptoms, the details of the loan, and the equipment's problem); and
- the respective *outcome* or *solution* (the verdict or ruling, the treatment, the outcome of the loan, and the technical fix).

Thus, a case typically comprises a problem and solution pairing. A collection of cases is called a case base, just as a collection of data records is called a database.

The problem and solution descriptions may be short or long depending on the area of knowledge in question. For example, the description of a property for sale may involve many parameters (such as lot size, number of rooms, garages, heating type), while the solution (the sale price) will be very short—just a dollar value.

Case bases divide into two broad categories:

- In *homogenous* case bases all cases share the same data or record structure; that is, cases have the same attributes but varying values.
- In *heterogeneous* case bases, cases have varied record structures; that is, cases may have different attributes and varying values.

An example of a homogenous case base would be one for a Realtor's office. Every house or case in the case base has exactly the same case structure; that is, the same fifty or so attributes are recorded for every property. It is relatively straightforward to identify a complete set of features, since all Realtors keep similar records of properties. Thus, it would be reasonable to assume that they will have already recorded necessary and sufficient information.

However, if the Realtor did not already have a property database, it would be easy to create a property case base. You would only have to think of the set of all features that could describe a property. This set can be reduced by considering only predictive features that affect property values. For example, the number of bedrooms and bathrooms are predictive of sale price, while the color of the carpets is probably not. Contextual information may also be of value here. For example, the state of the economy and the business cycle during the house sale may both influence the sale price. Interest rates and the plans of local major employers, for example, can have a profound effect on house prices. Tacit factors such as the "feel good factor" may play an important role but be hard to define and capture.

An example of a heterogeneous case base would be a patient diagnostic casebase. Patient records will contain a lot of information in common, such as age, blood type, and blood pressure, but also much information that is unique to each patient record, for example, medical history, treatments, and prognosis.

Cases cannot always be acquired from existing databases, and where good historical records do not exist, developers must elicit case features. This is a knowledge engineering task where the developer is seeking *feature stabilization*. This occurs when no new relevant case features can be identified either by challenging domain experts or by acquiring new cases.[1] This is likely to be much easier for homogenous case bases such as the Realtor's case base.

When developing a heterogeneous case base, developers may never be sure they have a complete feature set. For example, in a patient diagnostic case base, developers could not list *all* the possible medical conditions, symptoms, and tests a person could have. Thus, when developing a heterogeneous case base, it may be fruitless to imagine all possible features. Instead, developers must rely on historical records. If these are not available, developing a reliable

---

1 This process is described in the case study in Chapter 7.

case base will be difficult and will require extensive knowledge engineering.

The case studies that follow this chapter will highlight the distinction between these two types of case bases and the ease or difficulty of initially acquiring cases.

2.6 Case Storage and Indexing

Database systems use indexes to speed up the retrieval of data. For example, an index may be created to the family names of records about people in a database. An index is a computational data structure that can be held in memory and searched very quickly. This means the computer does not have to search each record stored on disk, which would be much slower. CBR also uses indexes to speed up retrieval. Information within a case is of two types:

- indexed information that is used for retrieval (this will tend to be explicit knowledge), and
- unindexed information that may provide tacit and contextual knowledge of value to a user but is not used directly in retrieval.

For example, in a medical system you may use a patient's age, sex, height, blood type, and weight as indexed features that can be used for retrieval, and you may include a photo of the patient as an unindexed feature. (See Figure 2.1.) The photo is not used for retrieval, but may be extremely useful in reminding medical staff who the patient is. (The photo helps remind staff of the full social context of the case.)

As a guideline, case indexes should:

- be predictive,
- address the purposes the case will be used for,
- be abstract enough to allow for widening the future use of the case base, and
- be concrete enough to be recognized in future.

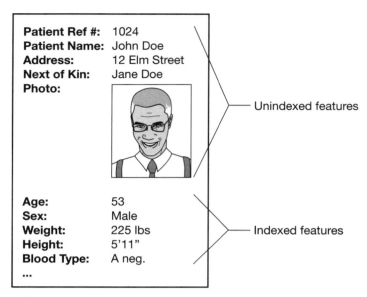

Figure 2.1   Indexed and unindexed case features.

Let us use the bank loan example again. Some information provided by prospective clients to you is clearly not predictive of their likely success at repaying a loan, such as their name or telephone number. Some information *may* be predictive, such as their address—if they live in an upmarket suburb, you might assume they are financially stable. However, certain information is clearly predictive of their ability to repay a loan; namely, their income and their existing financial commitments, such as home loans, car repayments, and life insurance. Thus, in this instance you may choose to use their income and financial commitments as your indexes since they are predictive, they address the purpose of the case base, they could be used for other purposes in future, and they are easily recognized.

2.7 Key Assumptions

Before progressing too far, it is a good idea to consider the assumptions that underpin case-based reasoning. A case-based reasoner makes some assumptions about the world in which it operates, and it is worth making these explicit before we continue. If these assumptions do not hold within your organization, a case-based reasoner cannot operate with any confidence.

2.7.1   The World is a Regular Place

A case-based reasoner assumes the world is regular; it cannot work in an irregular, random, or chaotic environment.

By this I mean that what holds true today will probably hold true to-morrow. If a fix was good for a problem yesterday, it is reasonable to assume it will be good for the same problem tomorrow. For example, if you have a headache, you may take an aspirin, and you do not expect it to make your headache worse because in the past it has usually helped.

2.7.2   Situations Repeat

A case-based reasoner expects situations to repeat. If they do not, there is no point in remembering them.

Presumably, one of the main reasons we bother to remember any-thing is because we believe the things we remember may be of some use to us in the future. When we encounter a problem such as getting the mower to start after the winter, getting the baby to go to sleep, or finding a parking space near that restaurant, we remember how we solved the problem in case it ever happens again. If situations do not repeat, there is no point in remembering them—a case base would be of no use.

2.7.3   Similar Problems Have Similar Solutions

Similar problems have similar solutions. If similar problems have very different solutions, a case-based reasoner may give inaccurate advice.

An aspirin can be taken for any mild pain, not just for a headache. Your special secret parking space is good for any place downtown near First and Main. Persuading the mower to start after the winter is much the same as getting the snow-blower to start after the fall.

Fortunately, these assumptions apply in our world most of the time, and so a case-based reasoner can be used with confidence in many different knowledge management application areas, as the case studies in the rest of the book show.

2.8 Conceptualizing CBR

You have seen that a case is a contextualized piece of knowledge representing an experience. It contains the past lesson that is the content of the case and the context in which the lesson can be used. A case can be an account of an event, a story, or some record typically comprising:

- the *problem* that describes the state of the world when the case occurred, and
- the *solution* that states the solution to (or outcome of) the problem.

One way this is often visualized is in terms of a *problem space* and a *solution space*. In Figure 2.2, you can see that an individual case is made up of two components—a problem description and a related solution. These can be thought of as residing, respectively, in the problem space and the solution space. The description of a new problem to be solved is positioned in the problem space. Retrieval identifies the case with the most similar problem description (the arrow labeled "R" in Figure 2.2), and its stored solution is found. If necessary, revision or adaptation occurs (the arrow labeled "A" in Figure 2.2), and a new solution is created. This conceptual model of CBR assumes that there is a direct one-to-one mapping between the problem and solution spaces. In other words, if a new problem is conceptually "down and to the right" of a known problem, then the new solution may also be "down and to the right" of the retrieved problem's solution.

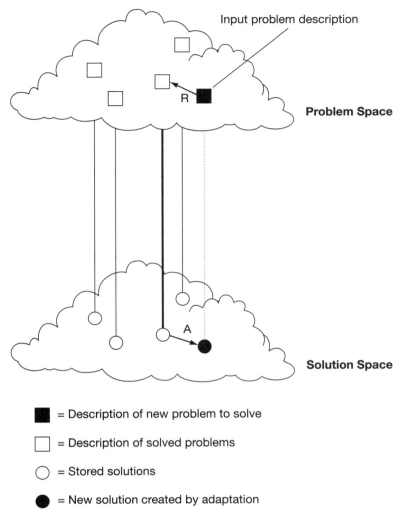

Figure 2.2   Problem and solution spaces (after Leake).[2]

2 Leake, D.B. (Ed.), 1996. *Case-Based Reasoning: Experiences, Lessons, & Future Directions.* AAAI Press/The MIT Press, Menlo Park, Calif.

Within a case, you can store most types of data that you would expect to be able to store in a normal database, for example, names, product identifiers, values such as cost or temperature, and textual notes. An increasing number of CBR tools also support multimedia features such as photos, sound, and video.

2.9 CBR Processes

Now we are ready to examine the six-REs—the six processes of the CBR cycle. Retrieval is given the most detailed treatment since it is at the core of all CBR systems.

2.9.1 Retrieval

When you have a requirement for knowledge—perhaps the solution to a specific problem you are dealing with—it is unlikely to be the same as those that have preceded it. Indeed, even if it were the same, you may not describe it the same way twice. Thus, you are interested in finding knowledge that is *similar* to your requirements. You are not looking for an exact match, although an exact match would be fine.

Most of the CBR systems described in the case studies use a retrieval technique called *nearest neighbor*. At a conceptual level nearest neighbor is very simple. Let us use the simplified bank manager example we introduced earlier, namely, how to decide if a new client should be granted a loan.

In this example, a case is a previous loan. First, let's decide on the case features we think appropriate. Two specific features seem suitable:

- a person's net monthly income (the money left after tax and after paying off other financial commitments), and
- the monthly repayment on the loan.

To simplify this explanation, let's use just these two features as indexes to our case base. Thus, our cases can be represented as shown in Figure 2.3.

The two indexes can be used as axes for a graph (see Figure 2.4), with net monthly income on the X-axis and monthly loan repayments on the Y-axis. A past case—for example, someone with a relatively high

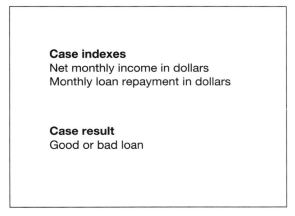

Case indexes
Net monthly income in dollars
Monthly loan repayment in dollars

Case result
Good or bad loan

Figure 2.3   A simple case representation.

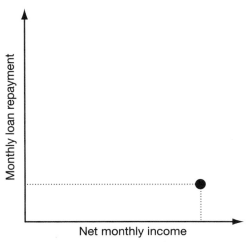

Figure 2.4   A simple graph for plotting loans.

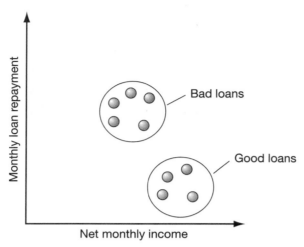

Figure 2.5   Clusters of good and bad loans.

net monthly income and a relatively low loan repayment—can be plotted on the graph.

In a similar way, other past cases can be plotted as points on our graph. Now, we said that our indexes should be predictive, and common sense tells us that people with relatively low net monthly incomes and relatively high loan repayments are more likely to default on the loan than those with high incomes and low repayments. Thus, it is no surprise if one of our clusters of cases represents those who successfully repaid their loans and the other represents those who defaulted, as shown in Figure 2.5.

We can now use this graph as a knowledge management tool. If a prospective client walks through the door, all we have to do is ask for her net monthly income, calculate the loan repayment, and plot this on our graph. If she falls in or near the *good* cluster, we should grant the loan. If she falls in or near the *bad* cluster, we should refuse the loan.

It is easy to see in Figure 2.6 that our new client is nearest the good loans. However, to be certain, we should use the graph to calculate the distances. All we need to do is to calculate the relative X and Y distance of the new case (the *target* case) to the other cases (the *source* cases). Let's

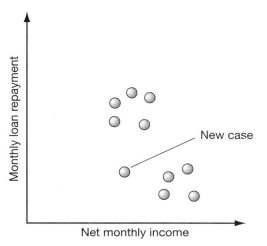

Figure 2.6   A new case on the graph.

simplify the graph and just consider three cases: two existing source cases called A and B and a target case called T. Let us also state that case A was a good loan and case B was a bad loan. We can now easily obtain an X and Y distance of T from each of the source cases A and B.

In Figure 2.7 the X distance of T from A is 3 units, and the Y distance is zero; while the X distance of T from B is 1 unit, and the Y distance is 3 units. Thus, we can say that:

The distance of T from A: $d_A = X_A + Y_A$
The distance of T from B: $d_B = X_B + Y_B$

Whichever gives the smallest value is the nearest neighboring case to T. Therefore, in our example, the distance of T from A equals 3 (3 + 0), while the distance of T from B equals 4 (1 + 3), and therefore A is T's nearest neighbor. You should recommend the loan. Although the target has a low income, the loan is also low. Our decision is supported by the nearest neighboring case (case A) being a good loan.

Nearest neighbor is that simple. However, we can make this more realistic by *weighting* the attributes. From your years of experience as a bank employee, you believe that a person's net monthly income is

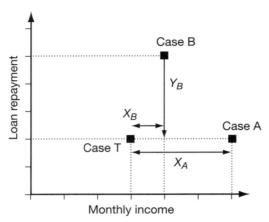

Figure 2.7   A graph with nearest neighbor distances.

more predictive of their ability to repay a loan than the relative size of the monthly loan repayment. Perhaps this is because people on high salaries tend to have more job security and financial stability than those on lower incomes. Let us say that we will weight the person's income as twice as important as the size of the loan repayment. We can still use the same graph, but our simple nearest neighbor formula changes to:

The distance of T from A: $d_A = (X_A \times W_X) + (Y_A \times W_Y)$
The distance of T from B $d_B = (X_B \times W_X) + (Y_B \times W_Y)$

where W_X is the weight of the attribute X, and W_Y is the weight of the attribute Y. We will state that $W_X = 2$ and $W_Y = 1$. Thus, the distance of T from A = 6, or $(3 \times 2) + (0 \times 1)$, and the distance of T from B = 5, or $(1 \times 2) + (3 \times 1)$.

Consequently, using our weighted nearest neighbor formula, case B is now the nearest neighbor to case T, and you should refuse the loan because case B was a bad loan. A way of visualizing this is to redraw the previous graph with the x-axis at twice the scale of the y-axis, as

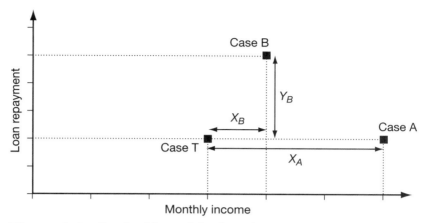

Figure 2.8   Graph with a weighted x-axis.

shown in Figure 2.8. This now more clearly shows that T is closer to B than to A.

You can see how adding background knowledge to our nearest neighbor formula in the form of relative importance or weightings on each attribute dramatically altered which case was retrieved as a best match.

Our example is very simple. In reality, cases may have ten, twenty, or more attributes, each with its own weighting. Instead of using a two-dimensional space, as in our example, cases are plotted into a *N*-dimensional space. Moreover, we are not restricted to simple numerical comparisons of similarity. Some case features may hold symbolic values (for example, the colors red, green, and blue), Boolean values (true, false, or unknown), and textual values.

Despite this increase in complexity, nearest neighbor algorithms all work in a similar fashion. For each attribute, the similarity (that is proximity) of the target case to a source case is determined. This measure may be multiplied by a weighting factor. Then the sum of the similarity of all attributes is calculated. This can be represented by the relatively simple equation:

$$Similarity(T, S) = \sum_{i=1}^{n} f(T_i, S_i) \times w_i$$

where:

T is the target case

S is the source case

n is the number of attributes in each case

i is an individual attribute from 1 to n

f is a similarity function for attribute i in cases T and S

w is the importance weighting of attribute i

Algorithms similar to this are used by most CBR tools to perform nearest neighbor retrieval. Similarities are usually normalized to fall within a range of zero to one (where zero is totally dissimilar and one is an exact match) or as a percentage similarity where 100 percent is an exact match.

OK, now you're asking, "Where's the tacit knowledge in this?" We could implement this system as an entirely explicit formalized mathematical model. You feed in the numbers and out comes the result: grant or refuse the loan. However, remember I said earlier that in a case, not all the case features are indexed or used by the retrieval system.

Some of the unindexed features may include important contextual information about the loan prospect like how long she has banked with you, whether her extended family also bank with you, how long she and her family have lived in the town and banked with you. This information might persuade you to think that she is a better loan prospect than the algorithm predicts. You may have a gut feeling that someone who has lived in your small town all her life is not going to default on a loan.

You will see in some of the case studies that this is a common feature of CBR knowledge management systems; namely, they retrieve contextualized knowledge (past cases) that helps people make better decisions. Yes this loan is a risk, but in your judgment a risk worth taking. You can even comment the case: "I've decided to grant the loan because the applicant, Jane Doe, and her extended family have lived in our town all their lives and also all bank with us. I don't think she will default on the loan." This could then be used in future to help others make decisions in similar circumstances.

2.9.2   Reuse

Once a similar case, or commonly, a set of similar cases, has been retrieved, the knowledge they contain can be reused. As you will see from most of the case studies in this book, the retrieved knowledge is most commonly applied or used by people. Only in some systems is the knowledge applied directly or automatically by the system itself.

I personally view it as a strength of CBR that people are kept in the loop. The CBR system does the work that people find hardest and least enjoyable—searching through past experience or knowledge, making comparisons, assessing similarity, and collating a list of similar cases—leaving people free to be creative in their application of the retrieved knowledge.

In our simple example, the reuse of the knowledge is the retrieval of similar loans suggesting that the loan should be refused, although there is evidence that the decision is borderline.

2.9.3   Revision

The use of knowledge often leads to revision of the knowledge. Sometimes if a past similar case is suggesting a solution, the solution needs some revision. Remember the problem and solution spaces and the statement "similar problems have similar solutions." I did not say similar problems have the *same* solutions. Many of the case studies in this book will show you that the CBR system retrieves past cases and people use the knowledge they contain to create new solutions. These new solutions are based upon adaptations of the retrieved solutions.

Once again, the CBR system performs the task that people find hard. Most of us do not like to solve problems completely from scratch. We like to be given an idea of what the solution looks like, something we can work with. A CBR system provides that support by giving us access to similar solutions to base our new solution on. Automatic solution adaptation is only performed in certain specialized areas and only where explicit knowledge is sufficient to solve the problem. You will see in the case studies that the majority of CBR systems do not perform automated solution adaptation.

In our example, the revision of the knowledge is the addition of the information to the case that the applicant and her extended family all have banked with the bank for many years. This indicates she is a good loan risk, and the decision is made to grant the loan. Her case is commented with the reason for the decision.

2.9.4 Review

Once a new solution has been generated, the outcome of the case should be reviewed. Was it successful? Could the outcome have been improved? This review process is an essential component of a CBR knowledge management system. You will see from the case studies that most of the case study systems have regular management meetings in which new cases are reviewed by a team of people. The outcome of the review process is a decision to retain the case as a new case in the case base, or not.

This process may also review the decisions that were made in controversial or marginal cases. In our banking example, the head office may override your decision, stating that "in the future the length of time a loan applicant's family has banked with us must not influence the decision to grant a loan." Conversely, the managers of the bank may agree that customer loyalty is an important asset, and similar loans should be granted in future similar situations.

What is important here is that the CBR-cycle, through its review process, provides an explicit way for decisions and their outcomes to be reviewed and for the knowledge they contain to be managed. We are not concerned here with the rights and wrongs of the way banks treat loyal customers.

2.9.5   Retain

The retention process involves adding the case to the case base. This may be as simple as adding a new record to the database, or it may involve some preprocessing of the case and even the acquisition of other supporting information and knowledge required to make the case complete.

It is worth noting here that the retention of a case is different from the retention of a database record. Our bank will of course retain records of every loan application in its databases. However, it may not necessarily keep every record in its knowledge management case base. Cases are retained because they contain valuable knowledge or lessons; they are not just records of every event or experience. Some case bases retain every instance, episode, event, or case, but many do not. Those that do not only retain high-value cases that act as exemplars or prototypes that can guide or inform decision makers in the future. The decision as to which cases should be retained is usually made by the management team.

2.9.6   Refine

Case bases are not static. They are not repositories of data that simply grow and grow. Instead, they acquire new knowledge as cases and equally may need to forget old or redundant cases. The world is a dynamic place, and what is true or useful today is not necessarily so tomorrow.

For example, people used to think that drilling holes in the skulls of patients with mental illness was a good cure. Today we prefer therapy and drug treatments. Just as we sometimes have to change what we hold as being true, so a case base must be refined. This process is called case-base maintenance, and it is not a trivial process. There are some automated tools under development in research laboratories to help with this activity, but commercial CBR tools do not yet provide much support for this other than providing statistics on cases in the case base and simple management functions and reports.

Consequently, this process is commonly subsumed under the review process described earlier. The same group of people that decide if a case should be retained also consider the following:

- Does the retention of a new case contradict or conflict with the knowledge contained in another case?
- Does the retention of a new case add to a large number of very similar cases in the case base that may be partially redundant?
- Does the new case indicate that a new feature has been discovered that usefully discriminates between some or all cases?
- Does the new case indicate that several existing features are facets of one feature? An obvious example of this is the banking example I used earlier. It is actually the ratio between income and loan repayment that is relevant.
- Finally, are there any cases in the case base that have become obsolete because of changes in knowledge or working practice?

Refinement of the case base is typically done periodically by the team responsible for maintaining the case base. If done diligently, it will ensure the continual evolution of the case base. If ignored, the case base's value will degrade with time.

2.10   Conclusion

By now, you should recognize that we all use CBR all the time to solve problems in our daily lives. We retrieve similar experiences from our memories, we reuse and revise the knowledge they contain, we review the lessons learned from new experiences and retain them, and over time, we refine our knowledge, constantly filtering and updating it.[3] Consequently, it makes sense that our knowledge management systems should use CBR as their core methodology.

It is not important that you completely understand how CBR systems are implemented. I have given you little technical information. Instead, it is only important that you are familiar with the six activities of the CBR cycle and understand what is involved in each one. You know what a case comprises, that it can contain both indexed and unindexed features, and that some case bases are uniform in case structure, like database records, while others are not. You should recognize when the assumptions of a case-based reasoner apply and when they may not, and hence be able to decide if your application area is suitable for CBR.

The following chapters describe seven case studies of knowledge management systems that all use CBR as their underlying methodology. The case studies range from large multinational corporations to small engineering firms, and they are drawn from across the globe and a variety of business sectors. Some of the case studies are very recent, while others were deployed many years ago and have been in long-term profitable use. The case studies were selected to exemplify different aspects of implementing a successful knowledge management system. As such they describe different facets of the implementation in different degrees of detail. Taken as a whole they provide an excellent insight into the deployment of knowledge management systems. The case studies described here were also selected to complement those in my previous book, and you should look there if you have a particular

---

3 Please note that I am not claiming that our minds use nearest neighbor retrieval to recall memories, but rather that our cognitive processes are similar or analogous to the CBR processes.

interest in applications of knowledge management to help desks and customer service.[4]

Finally, it is worth noting that each case study has been written by those involved directly with the project. Although I have edited them to ensure consistency of terminology, the authors' original voice and language have been retained. Some of the authors are employees of the organizations deploying the systems, and others are consultants employed to help implement the systems. Contact details for the authors are supplied in the Appendix, and they will be happy to provide further details of their systems on request.

At first, each case study will seem individual and unique. But as you read them, you should be able to recognize commonalities. In the final chapter, I will help you in this process by drawing together common themes from the case studies.

---

4 Watson, I. (1997). *Applying Case-Based Reasoning: Techniques for Enterprise Systems,* Morgan Kaufmann, San Francisco.

II

Case Studies

3

Managing Product Quality
Total Recall at National Semiconductor

Arthur Hamilton and Blaise Gomes
National Semiconductor

3.1 Introduction

National Semiconductor combines leading-edge analog and digital technologies to create highly integrated solutions for the information age. From complete systems on a single chip to high-performance multichip products and basic building blocks, National provides optimized solutions for the information appliance, personal computing, consumer, and communication markets. With headquarters in Santa Clara, California, National had annual sales of $2.1 billion in fiscal 2000 and about 10,500 employees worldwide.

A pioneer in the semiconductor industry, National Semiconductor was established in 1959. Since that time, the company has been at the vanguard of revolutionary electronics technologies, with achievements ranging from the design and manufacture of early discrete transistors to the introduction of a sophisticated integrated circuit product line. Today, National Semiconductor is an acknowledged leader in the design and manufacture of analog and mixed signal semiconductor products that provide access to the information highway.

3.2 The Problem

National has manufacturing sites around the globe. Its wafer fabrication facilities are located in Arlington, Texas; South Portland, Maine; and Greenock, Scotland. Test and assembly sites are in Malacca, Malaysia, and Singapore. From these sites, National ships hundreds of millions of semiconductor components to thousands of customers around the world. Out of all these shipments last year, customers returned approximately 4,000 individual parts where verified failures were analyzed. This corresponds to customer report defect rates of approximately thirty parts per million.

Although these numbers reflect the corporation's commitment to continuous improvement in reliability, today's marketplace depends on virtually perfect product reliability from semiconductor components. Being able to depend on deliveries with "zero defects" permits manufacturers to achieve lower costs in handling and testing of parts and helps "just in time" manufacturing schemes. The result is a higher overall value that provides a competitive advantage to National's customers.

Therefore, when the rare failure does occur, it is a cause of immediate concern for both National and the customer. In particular, the key concern is whether or not the failure is indicative of a manufacturing process that is moving out of control and if it might negatively impact the continuing reliability of the parts. To address this concern, and maintain confidence in products received from National, customers demand a rapid and complete failure analysis. Along with the analysis, customers look for corrective actions to be taken to ensure the root cause of any problem has been identified and that steps have been taken to guarantee it will not recur.

The advanced technology and complexity in today's semiconductors make this analysis a major challenge in its own right. To address it, National maintains a group within its Worldwide Quality Network that performs the Product Quality Analyses, or PQAs, that provide answers to anxious customers. This group is in turn supported by in-house analytical laboratories and engineers at worldwide sites. In total, National invests approximately $10 million annually in this function with personnel at eight sites around the world: the manufacturing sites named above as well as Santa Clara headquarters and major offices in Germany and Japan.

The technical and engineering talents of these people are not solely directed to failures that affect customers. They also participate in the development and qualification of new technology and processes, so their skills and knowledge also contribute to new products. Because of this, it is just as important to National to have these individuals complete customer PQAs quickly in order to focus more time and resources on the new development aspects of their work.

With both National and customers wanting to collect and process failure analysis data as quickly as possible, it is natural to look to some type of application software to support these efforts and help reduce cycle times.

3.2.1 Software Support

As technology has evolved, National has designed a progression of software support applications to aid the engineers and technicians in their work. Because National has adopted the Eight Discipline (8D) problem-solving methodology, originally defined by Ford Motor Company, recent support software has been structured on that model. This software is the Failure Analysis (FA) module of Aquaris (Advanced Quality and Reliability Information System).

The functionality of the Aquaris software focuses primarily on the production of the 8D reports that are delivered to the customer. The key information collected by the system is textual data describing the conclusions drawn during the analysis process. However, because the data is entered from locations around the world, there is usually little similarity in how the same conclusions are worded. While this text data can be manipulated to create the desired 8D reports, it does not contain sufficient information to describe the nature of the failure in a consistent manner.

Built around a Sybase database, Aquaris is accessed through an interface developed in PowerBuilder that requires a customer client to be installed on each user's desktop PC. Alternately, the data can be accessed through the customer client installed on National's thin-client network. Unfortunately, many users perceived the performance of the system to be slow. Because of this, they would accumulate information over a period of days and only update the database on a weekly basis. As a result, data was not in synch with the work being done, and status information passed on to customers was not necessarily current.

3.2.2 Application Upgrades

In late 1999, National began the task of upgrading the software support application to address the shortcomings of the system then in use. In particular, there were three main points to be addressed by the new application:

- better knowledge of the workflow involved in each PQA,
- more complete knowledge captured at each step of the analysis, and
- a Web-based client.

Better Workflow Knowledge

The new application software is designed to better recognize the various activities that occur during the analysis of a PQA. By recognizing the analysis activity that a PQA is currently undergoing, the application can produce status information that can be used for timely reporting. Customers will have better interim information on the status of the analysis. Management will be better able to identify bottlenecks in the PQA process so that resources can be allocated more effectively.

More Complete Knowledge

The system being replaced captured primarily the conclusions of the analysis. The new application provides the means to record not only textual information destined for 8D reports, but also information that would normally reside only in an engineer's lab book, where it would not be readily available for sharing with future analysts. This was particularly true of specific test results recorded on a device-by-device basis.

Web-Based Client

By changing to a Web-based client, the new application is available from every computer on the National Semiconductor intranet. It is expected that the improved speed and ease of access will encourage timely recording of PQA data. This will allow customers to gain real-time information on the status of the investigation under way on their behalf.

3.2.3   Knowledge Management and the Integration of CBR

At the same time work development began on the Aquaris FA module replacement, Barbara Maxham, Director of Quality Systems, mentioned a new technology she had heard briefly discussed, case-based reasoning. Barbara's experience had shown her that much failure analysis duplicated work that had been previously performed. This was not really surprising since, with eight worldwide locations and hundreds of people working on analyses, the earlier pertinent analysis was generally being performed somewhere else by someone else. The probability of not knowing about previous relevant work was high, as knowledge gained from the earlier analysis was not effectively shared. Although the 8D reports generated from previous work were available online in a "lessons learned library," there was no effective way to search this database.

In addition, searching the underlying database of the FA module was difficult. As mentioned earlier, the structure of the database did not account for specific test results, making it nearly impossible to search for earlier PQAs that exhibited "symptoms" similar to the current device under investigation.

Despite these difficulties, engineers would spend hours on Aquaris attempting to search for similar PQAs from the past, because it was the only tool available. When engineers were interviewed in order to understand how they used the system, they explained that they tried to look for previous PQAs that they vaguely remembered because of some similarity to their current analysis. Because they were attempting to retrieve a particular PQA, the search only focused on the range of PQAs with which they had been intimately involved. Searching for work done by others was seldom intentionally done.[1]

Naturally, users faced the same problem when searching a relational database with a standard search tool. The selection criteria were the logical "and"-ing of individual logical matches with whatever parametric values the user could muster. As could be expected, the set of information returned was often too large to be of use, or when the parameters were tightly defined, no matching PQAs were found.

It was here that the potential of CBR provided a perfect fit. It could find similar cases based on "having seen something like this before." This was precisely the approach taken by the engineers. However, while they only asked the question of PQAs on which they had worked, CBR could essentially ask this question of the entire database. In this way, CBR could better satisfy the desire to truly share lessons learned. The goal of accessing corporatewide experience could be realized.

---

1 You will see that the case study people are essentially already using CBR to solve problems. They are searching for similar PAQs in a library and hoping to reuse the problem-solving knowledge they contain. If people are already using a process analogous to CBR, it is a very good indicator that CBR can be successfully employed within a knowledge management system.

3.3 The Knowledge Management Solution

Barbara Maxham saw the development of the new FA module as the ideal time to consider adding CBR capability. If the module could capture the proper information for CBR to operate, it would have the potential to short-circuit a portion of a new analysis based on the findings of an earlier one. Work would not be duplicated when a similar failure came under analysis, cycle time would be reduced, and significant savings could be realized.

In particular, failure analyses often went through two levels, identified as FA1 and FA2. Basic information collected as a failure was verified in FA1. Often, based on the information alone, or less often, based on recognizing the failure signature, the PQA could be closed, and the proper corrective action taken. However, if the root cause of the failure could not be determined, the analysis went into the second phase, FA2. This was where more extensive and more expensive analysis was performed to understand the cause of the failure.

If CBR could reduce the percentage of PQAs that went into FA2, it would provide substantial savings in addition to helping reduce the cycle time in delivering responses to anxious customers.

The new integrated system was christened "Total Recall."

3.3.1 Expected Benefits

Referring to similar cases from the past allows FA engineers to short-circuit the analysis process and close cases based on earlier experience. With the old system, being able to find the proper earlier cases depended on the individual's experience, the chance matching of a distinctive characteristic of the earlier case during a database search, and sometimes luck. The methodical checking of the full database provided by CBR was expected to allow this short-circuiting to occur much more frequently. The full analysis work would not be needed.

As mentioned above, when this shortening of the process occurred, benefits would include reduced cycle time and the corresponding savings in cost. In addition to the immediate time and money saved, customers would be better served by faster response to their concerns, and their satisfaction with the company and product should improve. Finally, the resources spent on analyzing failures on past products could now be used to help designers understand issues that occurred during the development of new products.

The simple metric of cycle time is, of course, the primary measure of the system's effectiveness. However, the subjective response of engineers working with the system will also be a key determinant in deciding the level of success that can be assigned to Total Recall.

3.3.2 The Team

As a Fortune 500 corporation, National maintains a substantial IS division employing approximately 150 IS professionals. The major portion of the IS division focuses on issues related to corporate infrastructure and enterprise-level applications. Smaller groups dedicated to specific product lines and functional areas support specialized applications. One of these groups, managed by Mike Meltzer, was responsible for supporting the corporate quality organization and their needs. For example, it was this group that maintained the existing Aquaris system. In addition, they maintained the software supporting the online document control system, document control being a function managed by corporate quality. As such, Mike's group provided the primary development team for the project.

Corporate quality, referred to as "WQN" for Worldwide Quality Network, also maintained a small group whose focus was knowledge management for the quality organization. This group, managed by Blaise Gomes, included document control, and maintained the WQN pages on the corporate intranet. The group also had some software development capability and provided smaller informal applications needed by WQN, usually developing them in Lotus Notes. Blaise and another member of this group joined Mike's team to form the team for CBR development.

3.3.3   Implementation Plan

Because CBR was a new and unproven concept at National, it was felt that development of the new Failure Analysis Tracking module should not be dependent on CBR. The original implementation plan called for CBR to be essentially a "bolt-on" module with integration toward the end of the development. If CBR did not perform as advertised, its functionality would not be included in the application, or at least not in the initial rollout.

Therefore, initially there were two teams, albeit with some overlap of personnel, with one (PQA team) focusing on the workflow aspects of the failure analysis process and the other investigating CBR and available tools.

The PQA team had the advantage of being familiar with the FA module from the existing Aquaris system, and had a good feel for much of the information collected in the process of performing a failure analysis on a semiconductor product. However, effective tracking of the process meant that the source of that information, and the workflow that produced it, needed clarification. To get a clearer picture, the team conducted extensive interviews of Quality Assurance (QA) and Failure Analysis (FA) engineers involved in the work. This was done not only at the Santa Clara headquarters, but also at a number of remote sites, including Singapore, Malaysia, Maine, and Texas.

The team was hoping to be able to accurately define the proper workflow so that the application would not only be better able to track the status of each analysis, but also to guide the process and ensure the proper steps were being taken. In what became one of the development project's major challenges, the team found that there was no definable workflow process in the traditional sense.

It was relatively easy to define all the various steps through which an analysis *could* go, but there was no assurance as to the steps through which any individual analysis *would* go. While there were steps that almost every analysis would see, there were good reasons to allow the engineer to decide to bypass those steps. The team found that each analysis developed its own ad hoc workflow based on the availability of equipment, the engineer's experience, and a variety of other factors. The representation of the PQA workflow is discussed later in the chapter along with the description of the case representation.

While the PQA team was wrestling with the workflow problem, the CBR team was investigating this new technology. The factors that influenced and drove that choice are discussed later in the chapter. However, the decision to use structural CBR had an immediate impact on the implementation plan.[2]

The need to define the structure of the CBR case and the elements invited the merging of the two teams' efforts. The teams did merge, and the overall project received its new designation: Total Recall.

This milestone of sorts was followed by approximately ten weeks when the team met almost every day for working sessions, often lasting the entire day. They made decisions on how the structure of the PQA database could maintain compatibility with the existing database while adding the elements needed to provide the more detailed tracking ability required. They brainstormed ideas on what essential information would define a case and how it could be captured from the PQA database. From over 1,000 man-hours, the first full draft of the specification defining Total Recall emerged.

The specification stated that the CBR interaction would take place "under the covers" with all information programmatically forwarded to the CBR software. The mechanism to do this without user interaction was not clear. At the same time, there was still a considerable amount of mystery surrounding how CBR actually worked. The process of divining an appropriate similarity measure for an analysis under way seemed almost magical. The team decided they needed more detailed training in order to determine how to deeply integrate

---

2 Structural CBR refers to a CBR system where the case data model has internal structure, often using object-oriented representations as opposed to a flat database record–style case data model.

CBR into Total Recall and ensure the case modeling was going to be effective. A week's training for the entire team was arranged at the chosen CBR tool vendor's head office. Fortuitously for the team, that just happened to be in Paris!

The training helped expand the team's understanding in two key areas. The first was related to the techniques required to achieve the level of integration desired in using CBR to retrieve cases without user intervention in the query process. The second was further insights into the nature of the case model.

In order to move on this new understanding, the team again split into two subteams. One would focus on the development of the primary software to track PQA status and collect the needed information to create the query to be passed to the CBR software. The other would focus on refinement of the CBR case data model and the population of the initial case base.

They also concluded that when the data model was revised it would need to be tested prior to the availability of the PQA application. The quick development nature of Lotus Notes was leveraged to provide an online tool that allowed the collection of an initial case base and the loading of this case base into the CBR software so that the initial testing could be done. Over the summer of 2000 the initial case base information was captured, and the initial testing showed the type of case retrieval desired.

By early fall, the PQA functionality of Total Recall was available for introduction to selected users. Feedback was collected and a detailed plan put into place for the final segment of the development that included building administrative functions into the Total Recall system for CBR case management. A final refinement to the CBR model was implemented in late 2000 in the form of "don't care" segmentation (discussed later in the chapter).

Extensive training material was completed during February 2000 in preparation for the beta release. It was augmented with Lotus ScreenCam movies that provided a full audiovisual demonstration of system operation as well as segments on the overall system philosophy.

This gave users the experience of having a "system expert" available at all times to show each keystroke and mouse click needed to achieve any system function. This was distributed with the beta testing during March 2001.

Members of the team were deployed worldwide in early April 2001 when the system was rolled out. They provided in-person reinforcement of the training information provided in March and were available for assistance when the system changeover from Aquaris was made. Table 3.1 shows the timeline of the implementation plan.

Table 3.1   Total Recall project plan.

Date	Activity
Sep 1999	Initial PQA team formed
Oct 1999	Interviews of QA and FA engineers
Oct 1999	Review of CBR vendors
Nov 1999	Recognition of ad hoc workflow
Dec 1999	Merge of PQA and CBR teams
Feb 2000	Completion of first pass spec
Mar 2000	Extensive CBR training in Paris—divergence of team for focus
Apr 2000	Detailed CBR model (case representation) defined
May 2000	Notes tool for initial case capture
Aug 2000	Initial case base in place
Aug 2000	First functional Total Recall modules available
Sep 2000	Introduction of Total Recall to select users
Nov 2000	Definition of "don't care" segmentation
Jan 2001	CBR administrative functions defined for system
Feb 2001	Training material prepared
Mar 2001	Beta testing
Apr 2001	Worldwide rollout

3.3.4   Hardware and Software

The choice regarding a hardware platform was essentially predetermined. Virtually every desktop in the corporation has either a PC or UNIX workstation, sometimes both. Certain essentials of the software choice also were dictated by policy.

With an abundance of technically competent and computer-savvy employees throughout the corporation, the environment at National Semiconductor is such that there may be as many people generating software outside of the corporate IS group as within. Employees throughout the corporation often produce simple computer-based tools to help them in their everyday work. Sometimes the usage of these tools expands to include several engineers within a product line or division.

In general, this is beneficial because of how these small, often temporary, tools help the efficiency of a group of employees. It allows IS to focus on larger, more complex and sophisticated enterprise-level applications. Difficulties develop, however, when the tool usage grows, becomes integrated with a group's work, and the non-IS individual who created the tool, usually without documentation, leaves the group. IS is then expected to supply support and maintenance.

To help combat this, the IS group developed a policy that more rigorously defines the application environment that is supported. Two particular aspects that affected Total Recall were that all new applications be developed for access through a Web browser and that they use Sybase as the back-end database. In addition, approved development environments were basically limited to Silver Stream and Lotus Domino. Decisions on software development and tools were constrained by these parameters.

Selecting the CBR Software

A major software decision still open was the choice of how CBR would be integrated into the Total Recall application. Would the functionality be developed as part of the application, or could a commercially available tool be seamlessly integrated? As mentioned earlier, a separate team was formed to address this question and, if necessary, find a commercially available CBR tool.

The selection team was Mike Meltzer and Blaise Gomes, development managers from IS and WQN, respectively. They had worked together in the past to successfully introduce other leading-edge tools at National. From this past history they realized that the selection process should not be taken lightly. They realized the decisions they made would be a major factor in the overall success of the project and that a bad choice could haunt users for years to come.

Being novices with CBR, Mike and Blaise began an educational effort that included the usual web searches and trips to the library. Two books proved very useful during this initial research.[3,4] While these texts were invaluable in providing knowledge of the nature and nuances of CBR, the team knew from experience there was no substitute for the information that can be gained through personal contact and dialogue with active practitioners of CBR.

The next step was to develop a requirements document. Again, past experience dictated that this was done early in the process, as it enabled the team to develop questions pertinent to the selection. It provides a basis for intelligent dialogue with potential CBR software suppliers and a way to objectively evaluate new technologies, tools, and suppliers by ensuring that all are measured on a level playing field.

The document included a broad range of business as well as technical evaluation criteria. Each criterion was also tempered with three supporting factors: *importance, priority,* and *timing*. Having these well-defined criteria prevented the selection process from deteriorating into

---

3 Watson, I. (1997). *Applying Case-Based Reasoning: Techniques for Enterprise Systems,* Morgan Kaufmann, San Francisco.

4 Bergmann, R., Breen, S., Göker, M., Manago, M. & Wess, S. (1999). Developing Industrial Case-Based Reasoning Applications: The INRECA Methodology. Lecture Notes in Artificial Intelligence, LNAI 1612, Springer Verlag.

a comparison of marketing hype from each of the competing software suppliers and consultants. The key criteria included in the requirements document are listed here:

- Architecture
- Client/server support
- Client platforms
- Server platforms
- Network topologies
- RDBMS compliance
- Published API
- Support for standard
- Scalability and performance
- Integration with third-party applications
- Web interface
- Customization
- Modeling
- Transferability of knowledge and ownership
- Cost of software
- Maintenance
- Case base development
- Total cost of ownership
- Return on investment
- Supplier stability
- Supplier vision
- Supplier direction
- Track record

The next step in the selection process was the identification of potential software suppliers and consultants. Mike and Blaise identified six promising candidates and started a dialogue with each. The requirement criteria were continually refined as the team's knowledge and understanding of CBR grew. The field was then narrowed to three suppliers. Each was given a copy of the requirements document and a sample of data from the current system. They were given an opportunity to manipulate the data provided and demonstrate what search results were possible. During visits and discussions, the team observed and evaluated the case-base development process as well as the product interface.

This round of supplier evaluation provided an unexpected insight that had a significant impact on the development of the entire project. Seeing how the suppliers worked with the data exposed a surprising weakness. The team believed the failure analysis data from the current Aquaris system had been fairly well structured and in good condition. The reality was considerably different. The exercise with the suppliers illustrated a considerable lack of consistency in the way failure analysis information was conveyed. This was traced back to the relatively free-form way engineers had been allowed to record the findings of their analysis. It also helped explain why conventional database searches of the existing database had been so ineffective.[5]

In addition to extensive contact with potential suppliers, Mike and Blaise contacted a selected group of the suppliers' current customers who were at different stages of their implementation of CBR. Their experiences helped the team identify possible obstacles and pitfalls that might, and would, be encountered both technically and culturally. They provided a wealth of knowledge and ideas, and their inputs became very instrumental in the way National approached development efforts. While this information helped refine the final revisions of the requirements document, the enthusiasm they expressed for CBR also found its way back to the development team.

---

5 This is remarkably common. Developers of CBR systems often assume that because records exist they can easily be translated into cases. Unfortunately, as several case studies here show, this is often not so. Existing records are often incomplete, noisy, and ambiguous and typically require augmenting before they make good cases.

A key factor leading to the final supplier choice was the decision to use structural CBR over conversational or textual CBR.[6] Despite discovering difficulties with the data model used in Aquaris, the team still felt that the structural approach best matched the type of data produced during the failure analysis process. In addition, the team concluded that maintenance of the resulting extensive case-base would be more economical over the long haul using structural CBR.

The eventual choice that came out of the evaluation process was to use the CBR tool offered by Kaidara.[7] A key factor that weighed heavily in Kaidara's favor was the basic philosophy and approach that they endorsed regarding the initial development of National's CBR usage in Total Recall. They would be available for extensive consulting early in the development while transferring knowledge and tools to enable National to take over, maintain, and further develop the application.

An initial concern was the distance that separated National's new French partners from the development team in California. Regular visits from Kaidara personnel, as well as the extensive training received in Paris, helped build a true partnership between the companies. In addition, about midway through Total Recall's development, Kaidara opened an office in Palo Alto, California, offering even more local support.

3.3.5   System Architecture

The overall system can be viewed as consisting of four servers and the Web client, as shown in Figure 3.1. Here is a basic description of each component:

---

6   Conversational or textual CBR systems use a natural language query to retrieve cases from a case-base that has a textual case representation (similar to a database record). Once a set of similar cases has been retrieved, a question and answer process (a conversation) is initiated by the CBR system to narrow down the set of similar cases to a small number of most similar cases.

7   Contact details of CBR tool vendors are given in the Appendix.

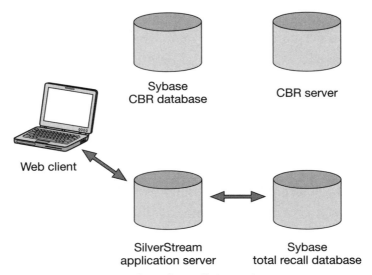

Figure 3.1 Normal Total Recall Operation.

■ *Silver Stream application server.* The main server for the application provides data manipulation functions and presentation to users.

■ *Total Recall database.* This database maintains all data collected and produced related to PQA processes.

■ *CBR database.* A separate Sybase database contains CBR representation of cases, including mapping information that relates case "footprint" numbers to specific devices analyzed during PQA processing.

■ *CBR server.* This is the home of the finalized case base and CBR engine.

The usual operation of the Total Recall application involves only the Web client interacting with the Total Recall database through the Silver Stream application server. In this mode the user is entering data related to the failure analysis under way. The database is collecting the observed results from the testing performed under a number of PQA-

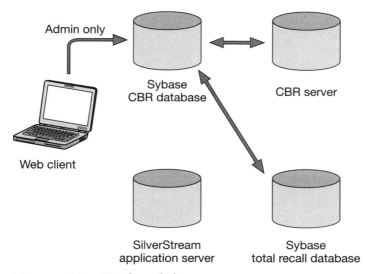

Figure 3.2   CBR knowledge management.

related activities. This provides all the information needed to determine the status of any PQA.

The CBR portion of the application is structured as shown in Figure 3.2.

Pertinent data from the Total Recall database is manipulated to create a case representation that is provided to the CBR database. Here this data is filtered further via administrative functions to create the complete case base. This case base is then periodically uploaded to the CBR server where it is queried via the Kaidara CBR engine to conduct searches. Figure 3.3 illustrates manipulation of the data in the CBR database.

As discussed further in Section 3.3.9, not all PQAs produce new cases for the CBR case base. A "nomination" process has been developed that brings potential cases to the CBR database where the case base administrator decides their fate.[8] A subset of the nominated

___

8 This is the review process of the CBR-cycle.

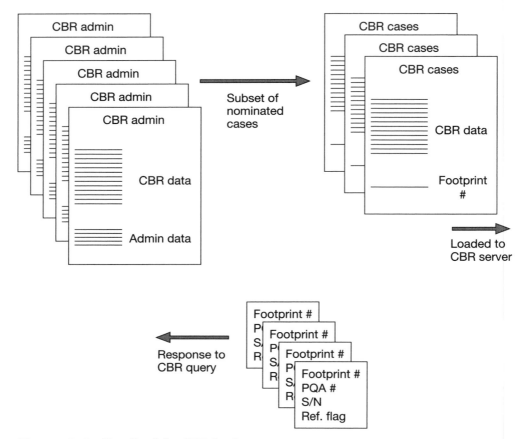

Figure 3.3   Details of the CBR database.

cases becomes a part of the CBR case base that is searched during queries. An assigned footprint number becomes the key identifier of each case. A footprint represents the observed characteristics of a failure in a single device that has been analyzed during the PQA process.

Other devices on other PQAs may have failed in a similar way. Rather than treat these as separate cases, they are considered "refer-

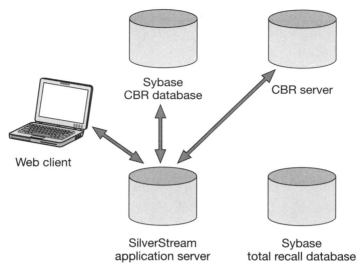

Figure 3.4   A CBR query.

ence" cases. The same footprint number is also used to identify these reference cases.[9]

When a CBR query is made, it is made from the Silver Stream application to the Kaidara CBR engine. It responds with a set of footprint numbers that represent the set of cases similar to the case in the query. This is shown in Figure 3.4.

With this set of footprint numbers, the application can search the CBR database and translate the footprint number into the PQA number and serial number (S/N) of the individual device with which users are more familiar. In addition, the system returns the PQA and S/N numbers associated with the reference cases related

---

9 Remember I said in Chapter 2 that most CBR systems do not retain every episode or case but rather retain only valuable cases that have knowledge to impart. The technique of referencing very similar cases described here is an efficient way to implement this retention policy.

to the main footprint case. In this way users can refer to several reports for hints and ideas about a solution to the problem they are currently facing.

3.3.6 Case Representation

A key piece of information garnered from current CBR users during the evaluation of potential CBR software suppliers was the importance of a good case data model. The accompanying warning that it might take multiple attempts before we got it right proved prophetic. It did indeed require several iterations before a satisfactory model was fully developed. The time spent doing this was worthwhile and helped identify and find solutions to potential shortcomings in the system before release. It was also an intriguing exercise that made the development team examine the work processes involved with failure analysis in unique ways.

There were two significant modeling issues to be addressed in the design of the Total Recall system. One was, of course, the case data model, and the other was how a PQA would be modeled. Because CBR was to be invoked programmatically from within the context of the PQA tracking system, it was important that the two models work in concert. It was necessary for the analysis data captured by the PQA system to be the data needed to create the query to the CBR system.

This was complicated by the fact that the workflow for the failure analysis could not be accurately defined in any traditional sense. The variables that went into an analysis created what was eventually referred to as an ad hoc workflow. This meant that neither model could depend on a fixed set of information on which to work. The models needed the flexibility to address this.[10]

---

10 Here we see the developers encountering the problems of making knowledge explicit and codifying it. They could attempt to formalize the workflow, but this would be an act of artifice. It would not capture what actually happened in practice, and tacit knowledge would be lost. A flexible case data model could capture the ad hoc nature of the workflow, whereas techniques like business rules could not.

Workflow Model

The workflow model that emerged took the list of possible steps and identified those as potential *activities*. The way tracking was done in the system was to record the sequence of the actual activities that were performed during the analysis. These activities, listed below, typically represent the types of tests and examinations the devices undergo.

- Initialization
- External visual
- Bench mechanical
- Curve trace
- ATE testing
- Bench testing
- Stress testing
- Stress analysis
- Post-stress curve trace
- Post-stress ATE testing
- Post-stress bench testing
- X-ray
- SAT/SAM
- Decap and inspect
- Deprocess and inspect
- Cross-section and inspect
- Light emission microscopy
- Liquid crystal analysis
- EBIC
- Probing and isolation
- Elemental analysis

This list is extended with other actions that do not contribute directly to the analysis, but are needed to allow the system to track the status of any PQA. These "pseudoactivities" include actions such as parts being shipped from one location to another, parts waiting for consultation, and other administrative functions.

Clearly, performing a test is not useful unless the result of that test is recorded. In Total Recall these results are referred to as *observations*.

The system captures these observations and maintains the relation between the observations and the activities and devices from which they came. The set of observations collected from any single device under analysis represents the basic information that describes the device's failure. This then provides the information that can be passed in a query to the CBR engine to see what similar cases might exist in the case base.

Initially, it seemed obvious that there would be a simple mapping between the PQA model and the CBR data model. Each PQA activity corresponded to a CBR attribute. The observation related to the activity would become the value of the attribute. Unfortunately, the reality was not that straightforward.

The major problem with this simple mapping was related to the same circumstances that forced the ad hoc workflow. One reason the FA engineer had such a plethora of activity choices was that there were multiple ways to gather the same essential piece of information. For example, a specific parametric failure might be detected while a part was being tested on automated test equipment as part of an ATE activity. However, if that part is being analyzed at a site that is not equipped with the appropriate piece of equipment, or if that equipment is being used for other purposes, the engineer might decide to perform a bench test activity and discover the same parametric failure.

It is clear that the parametric failure is the critical piece of information that must be compared for similar failures in the CBR case base. But the simple mapping function would relate the test result to one activity and attribute (ATE), while the second would relate the result to a different activity and attribute (bench test). A CBR search would not recognize the similarity between the distinct attributes.

Consider another example in which some locations use an X-ray activity to provide an initial view of the internal state of the device being analyzed. Other sites might choose to perform a chemical decapsulation activity to obtain an internal view. The same detected defect, if related to different CBR attributes with a simple mapping scheme, would not produce the desired similarity.

Table 3.2   CBR domain attributes.

Static Attributes	Dynamic Attributes
Customer special	Customer claim
NSID	Failure location
Parent die	Reported fail temp.
Family code	Continuity
Technology	Parametric
Fab process	Functionality
Package	Failure condition
Leads	Post-stress continuity
Date code	Post-stress parametric
Fab location	Post-stress functionality
Assembly location	Post-stress failure condition
Die rev	Stress analysis
Customer name	Package integrity
Customer location	Exposing
Device type	Fault isolation
	Detecting
	Case type

In other words, the data model developed with the failure analysis model in mind did not fit our knowledge management requirements. Therefore a second model was developed that represented the essential nature of the observation made, independently of how it was observed. The elements of this second model were the CBR attributes.[11] These are shown in Table 3.2.

---

11 This is not an uncommon experience. As mentioned before, even when records exist, it is common to find that because they have been kept for other purposes, they do not serve a knowledge management function without alteration. For example, troubleshooting tickets for equipment often record the reported symptoms or defect, the time the engineer was called out, and the replacement parts that were fitted. What they often do not record is the actual fault and its potential cause.

The eventual data model would have two distinct domains: one described in terms of PQA activities and their related observations, the second, a CBR domain described in terms of generalized attributes and their related values. The last step was to define a mapping function that understood both the PQA domain and the CBR domain and could map a PQA-oriented observation into a value related to a CBR-oriented attribute.

This mapping function decoupled the two domains, allowing any workflow issues that might arise at an individual site to be addressed without impacting the CBR data model. Any departure from the "expected" workflow would be handled within the mapping function. The result is that the "dual domain" model allowed unique approaches to performing the analysis and the resulting ad hoc workflow to continue to make use of CBR functionality.

A simplified schematic of the mapping function is illustrated in Figure 3.5. The analysis-oriented observations made during PQA activities are mapped into the essential values of the related CBR attributes.

Local Similarity and Data Types

The task of defining the case data model did not stop here. Because the similarity between two cases is calculated as a weighted sum of the local similarity between the attribute values, the data modeling is not complete until consideration is given to that local similarity function.[12] In this project, that task presented some interesting challenges in its own right.

The most significant issue to address involved the static attributes, identified in Table 3.2. These static attributes essentially describe the device that failed independent of the failure. They represent the identification of the device in terms of any part numbers associated with it, the technologies and processes in which it was built, where and when it was built, and so on. These attributes are distinguished from the

---

12 This is the nearest neighbor algorithm described in Chapter 2.

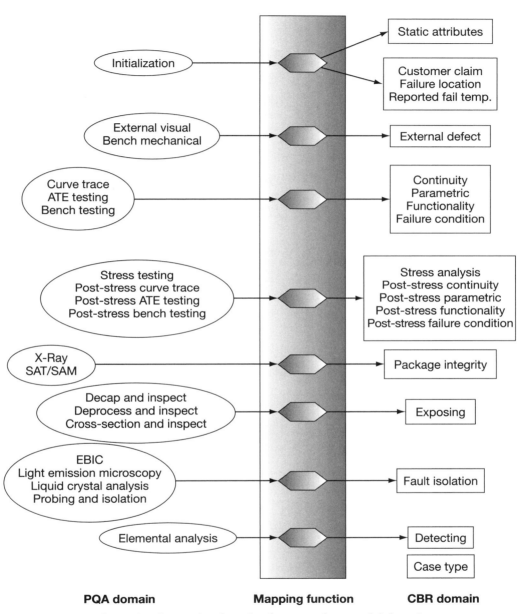

Figure 3.5   Schematic of mapping function between data model domains.

dynamic attributes, which represent that information discovered as the analysis progressed.

A basic assumption made in defining the data model was that similar devices would often fail in similar ways. Therefore, it was desirable to recognize this similarity and favor accessing past failure analyses on such similar devices. This was particularly true early in the analysis when little, if any, dynamic information was available. This would occur when the failure was first reported. It would allow an early screening of past PQAs that might have been done on "similar" parts in the past.

The challenge was how to structure the CBR model to recognize this device similarity. Ideally, all devices offered by the company would be listed in a massive taxonomy that would include all the various aspects of the device. A single piece of data, the part number, would be all that was needed to convey all the information inherent in its nature. This approach soon failed. With thousands of devices offered by National Semiconductor, the initial effort in defining the structure would be as large as the entire application effort. In addition, maintaining such a structure as new parts were introduced would be as large a task as managing the case base itself.

The team then compromised by ensuring that the list of static attributes captured the full range of dimensions in which parts could vary. These individual attributes were largely derived from a single piece of information: the part number. However, each would be treated as a single valued symbolic attribute, and each would contribute independently to the overall similarity between parts.

The result was what the team eventually referred to as "cumulative hierarchical similarity." For example, if two identical parts were compared, all thirteen device-related attributes would be 100 percent similar, and the full force of the similarity would be realized. If it was the same basic device in a different package, perhaps eleven or twelve of the related attributes would be identical, and the total similarity would be close to 100 percent. If the devices were perhaps two different amplifiers built in the same process, the similarity would be slightly less. If the devices were still two amplifiers, but built in different processes (such as bipolar and CMOS), there would be yet another reduction in the similarity contribution.

With this understanding, the model was able to use data types that would be easier to manage throughout the life of the application, but would still account for the multidimensional nature of device similarity.

What's Important?

In developing the data model for the case representation, a distinction was recognized between a CBR case base and a traditional relational database. CBR introduces the concept of the *relative importance* of each attribute when examining cases for similarity.[13] By applying importance weighting to each attribute, the result of a query can be manipulated and fine-tuned to produce the most meaningful results. However, when considering what the allocation of weighting factors should be, it seemed that every scenario put forth arguing the importance of one set of attributes produced another scenario arguing the importance of others.

Typically the determination of weighting factors is either fixed or can be varied during the query of the case base. This is reasonable when the query is a search to help a selection. The user making the selection knows what is important to him. For example, consider a CBR application to help a user select a particular semiconductor. The CBR application might maintain attributes such as power dissipation limits, package type, bandwidth gain, and price. The user making the query has all the knowledge necessary to assign an importance weighting to each attribute. He knows what he wants to pay, what power his system can handle, and what gain is needed.

However, in a failure analysis application this flexibility does not appear to work as well. Consider the data model described above that

---

13 The concept of weighting case features or attributes to reflect their relative importance was discussed in Chapter 2.

has attributes related to customer identification, device identification, electrical parametric failures, and visually detected defects. The user, by definition, doesn't know the cause of the failure, which is why the analysis is being done. It might be due to fabrication problems, assembly errors, or customer misuse. Hence, the user has no way to weight the different attributes, except to guess.

On the other hand, the cases in the case base have been completed. They inherently have the knowledge as to what is important. Because the root cause of the failure has been determined when the PQA was completed, which attribute or set of attributes is important can be determined when the case is entered into the case base.

For example, assume it is clear that misuse by a particular customer might contribute to failures seen over a period of time. In this case it is appropriate to include customer identification as an attribute that would increase the similarity between cases related to the same customer. However, with this attribute included in all cases, the lack of similarity in this attribute causes an effective lowering of scores between cases that are not affected by who the customer was. Conversely, if a case where the customer doesn't play a role in the failure carries the customer identification, the similarity to other cases related to the same customer results in a higher, undeserved similarity based on coincidence. In either scenario, there are sets of cases where the customer identification plays no useful role in the model.

Thus, the proper place for this weighting intelligence to reside seems to be in the case rather than in the query. For this example, in those cases where the customer played a significant role in the failure, the weighting of the customer-related attributes would be higher. In those cases that were not affected by the customer, the weighting of that attribute should be zero. In essence, the treatment of that attribute should become a "don't care" condition for those cases in which it played no role.

This conclusion created two significant problems. The first was that a considerable burden would be placed on the case base administrator if custom weighting had to be developed for each attribute in every new case to be added to the case base. The second and more immediate concern was that the CBR software did not support variable weighting by the case.

A compromise was reached that addressed both problems. The concept of a "don't care" condition was addressed on a simplified group of attributes rather than each individual attribute. Specifically, three categories were defined that would group appropriate attributes and treat the entire group as a "don't care." This simplifies the task for the administrator, who will not be responsible for developing a full set of attribute weights for each case. All that has to be done is to identify the case within these broader categories through the "case type" pseudoattribute. It is an encoded value that represents the "don't care" classification of the case and is not used directly in the calculation of the CBR similarity.[14]

Working closely with Kaidara, an enhanced module was created that implemented this logic into their CBR tool. The result is that the "don't care" classification essentially removes the related attributes from the model. The similarity function shows zero similarity, and the importance weighting of the attribute is also reduced to zero for the identified attributes. Therefore, the attributes do not add to the similarity, nor do they reduce the similarity score by adding to the total weight.

3.3.7   Case Acquisition

One of the project's more difficult tasks was the population of the initial case base. As mentioned earlier, the data in the legacy system was not well structured and could not be accurately accessed programmatically. The written report generated for each potential case had to be individually reviewed and the data augmented and cleaned up prior to being manually entered into the system.

---

14 In other words, it is an unindexed attribute.

This task also became a significant cultural obstacle. Because each potential case had to be reviewed on a technical level, the assistance of failure analysis engineers was needed. Asking them to take a sufficient amount of time from their busy workloads to work on a system under development that they did not fully understand proved to be a problem. Even after several attempts, only limited success could be claimed.

Over the summer of 2000 an intern from Kaidara consulted on a full-time basis. He was teamed with a summer intern from a Teacher Fellowship program sponsored by National. These two individuals took on the unenviable task of reworking hardcopy reports from the Aquaris system into suitable input for the CBR case base. They performed the bulk of the data extraction and conversion, consulting with the original engineer as needed. Out of this effort came refined lists of observation choices for the various PQA activities and mapped values for the CBR attributes.

To assist them in this work, a Lotus Notes database was created that would put this data online. A Notes form would be created that would allow the information from the initial analysis of the PQA report to be entered. If additional clarifying input was needed from an engineer, the form could be updated online at the engineer's convenience. After this PQA-oriented description of the case had been entered, the Notes program performed the mapping and presented the description appropriate for the CBR domain. While this was a time-consuming and sometimes painful process, it did lead to the final syntax used in the system. Eventually the intern team, working with the case base administrator, developed a comfortable process with which they could evaluate potential new cases, determine whether additional values for observations and attributes needed to be defined, and slowly build the initial case base.

When the process was running smoothly, an invitation was given to all QA and FA engineers to identify several PQAs that they thought were interesting and would make good cases. This provided the case base with another group of cases.

Approximately 200 cases were collected and formed the basis of the initial case base. This was barely enough to do the initial testing. The size of the case base can be expected to grow quite rapidly during the initial use of Total Recall. Fortunately, due in part to the work described here, Total Recall will have the structured data available to make the addition of new cases a much easier proposition.

In retrospect, a more intensive education process for the engineers might have made it easier to gain their participation in the initial population of the case base. Although the time taken away from their work for training seemed excessive at the time, it might well have paid dividends in the size and quality of the case base.

3.3.8   Case Retrieval

As discussed earlier in Section 3.3.5, the experience gained from performing PQAs is stored in the total CBR database as a series of footprint and reference cases. When a CBR query is made from the Total Recall system, it is relayed to the CBR server. Its response is an ordered set of cases sorted by declining similarity.

With these cases identified by the footprint number, the Total Recall application makes an additional search of the CBR database to translate these footprint numbers into the PQA and device serial numbers that are more meaningful to the user. In addition, PQA and serial numbers of reference cases are captured. This information then allows QA and FA engineers to retrieve, online, the final 8D reports corresponding to these earlier PQAs.

From this point it is the task of the engineer/user to peruse the 8D reports and decide whether the failure mechanism and corrective actions described for these earlier failures apply to their current situation. It is the responsibility of the engineer to either adopt or adapt the earlier findings.[15]

---

15 This is both the reuse and revise processes of the CBR-cycle.

3.3.9 Case Retention

When users close a PQA—that is, when the analysis is complete—they have the opportunity to nominate the PQA for inclusion in the case base as a new case. This nomination process provides the main means by which new cases are added to the case base.

At the conclusion of the PQA, the user, because hindsight is 20/20, is thoroughly aware of the nature of the failure. The system attempts to take advantage of this knowledge by allowing the user to more thoroughly refine the description of the case. This is done by showing an editing screen where the user can filter any irrelevant analysis. This will also allow the case to be marked so that the proper case type classification can be assigned to address the "don't care" situation described in the discussion of the data model.

It is then the task of the case base administrator to perform the final evaluation of the nominated case. The administrator searches the case base to check the similarity of the nominated case to existing cases. The goal is not to have numerous examples of similar cases in the case base in order to avoid overwhelming users with an unwieldy set of retrieved cases when doing a search. Based on this evaluation, the case base administrator will make the decision to treat the newly nominated case as a new footprint or as a reference case to an existing case. He or she could also decide to make the new case the footprint while "demoting" the existing footprint case to reference status.

Provision is also made for the case base administrator to involve the QA/FA engineers in a technical review board to further evaluate cases and make a final determination.[16]

---

16 As discussed in Chapter 2, the review, retain, and refine processes of the CBR-cycle have been subsumed into a single process. This is quite common, but it is worth remembering that three separate tasks are being done.

3.3.10   Interface Design

The Failure Analysis module of Aquaris heavily influenced the interface to the entire Total Recall system. Where possible, Total Recall duplicated much of the structure of the Aquaris screens, adapting them to meet the idiosyncrasies of the Web environment and adding the capability to capture new information such as activities and the explicit related observations.

3.3.11   Testing

Testing was done using Kaidara's standalone CBR application. It allowed cases to be entered via Excel spreadsheets that were, in turn, produced from the Notes system developed to capture the initial case base. From there, subject matter experts provided different levels of data, simulating the collection of data that would occur during the normal PQA process.

Results were consistent with the known cases within the database. The results were relatively easy to correlate due to the rather small initial case base. Individuals familiar with the cases that had been loaded confirmed that the results were consistent with the known cases within the database. They were also able to modify the query to move it away from a known solution that was in the case base and confirm the lowering of the similarity score returned.

3.3.12   Rollout

With sites around the world using this application, rollout was approached with a great deal of care. Having previously launched applications to this worldwide audience, experience dictated many of the steps that were taken.

Proper training before the launch was a key issue. The general nature of the system was well known since it was a replacement for the Aquaris Failure Analysis module. The concept of recording the sequence of PQA activities, the structured capture of observations made, and the look and feel of the Web-based interface were the primary operational aspects that had to be conveyed to users. Because CBR was operating in the background, there was little that impacted the training in terms of its operation in the system. However, a good deal of training was needed in terms of the CBR concept and how it could help users.

Over the year preceding the launch, the team took advantage of every opportunity to offer presentations on CBR at any venue where QA and FA engineers met, including their annual worldwide forum. In addition, when any team member traveled to another National site, the latest CBR presentation was brought along. To provide a status update on the entire project and reinforce the concepts behind CBR, videoconferences were held with the most remote sites at various stages during the application development.

In addition, Lotus ScreenCam movies were made of the operation of all phases of the system. These movies provided a keystroke-by-keystroke, click-by-click demonstration of the system accompanied by an audio description. CDs were burned with these movies and distributed to users before the launch of the system. They served both as an immediate training aid and a companion piece to the system documentation. A main advantage was that users, particularly those with English as a second language, could replay portions of the movie as often as needed to fully understand the operation.

Finally, the week of the launch, team members traveled to all the remote sites to do a final presentation, answer any questions, and be on hand when the "switch was thrown." In this way an on-site representative supported users at the most critical moment. Users were not left with the feeling that a software tool had been thrust upon them.

3.4 Conclusion

The development of the Total Recall application shared characteristics of many other development projects: everything took longer than expected, the development was more difficult than expected, and the users changed their minds about what they wanted to see too often. While that statement is somewhat facetious, the aspects of the normal delays and difficulties related to the CBR portion of the application offer some interesting insights.

Certainly the most obvious is the difficulty in forming the data model for the case representation. Considerable discipline is involved in breaking down the existing processes and examining the related information to determine what is really essential. It can be useful to approach the problem as a philosopher and ask about the essence of the problem rather than attempt a blind description of its external characteristics. In Total Recall the data model underwent two or three "fresh starts" and numerous refinements after the "final" structure was adopted. A key factor in determining the architecture of the system was the recognition that nothing should be hard-coded into the model and that the modification and addition of future CBR attributes should be easy to do.

This push for close examination extended beyond the CBR model and was focused on the PQA process as well. In the description of the case representation, the team found the need to take a different view of workflow and recognize what was needed to accurately handle the wide range of variation that was found. The team took the position that the software had to adapt to the workflow rather than overly dictate to users the way they should do their job. The discipline demanded by CBR conditioned the team to be more amenable to this position than they might be otherwise.

"The Quality Policy at National Semiconductor is to continuously improve our processes, products, and services to deliver solutions of the highest value," notes Jim Gordon, Vice President of the Worldwide Quality Network. "Even if CBR does not deliver fully on its promise of vast savings in time and money, the involvement with it has helped direct us to a closer look at our existing processes. In doing so, our understanding has improved and the failure analysis process along with it."

The fact that CBR was integrated so deeply within the system also made the development task more difficult than it might have been. Rather than use it as a freestanding tool, the desire to programmatically generate queries and translate responses required a substantial effort in its own right. It also required working very closely with the CBR software supplier, Kaidara. Anyone embarking on a CBR development should ensure they have the strong support of their CBR software supplier. Particularly, if CBR is a new technology, as it was in Total Recall, the assistance offered by an involved supplier cannot be underestimated.

Evaluation of the usefulness of CBR in this application is still to come, but the promise it offers can be expected to be included in future developments at National Semiconductor. Another active program is using it on the company's external Web site to help customers select devices that most closely meet their circuit needs. It is also being considered as an enhancement when the next Aquaris module is converted to Web usage.

4

Developing Expertise
Color Matching
at General Electric Plastics

William Cheetham and John Graf
General Electric Company

4.1 Introduction

General Electric (GE) traces its beginnings to Thomas A. Edison, who established the Edison Electric Light Company in 1878. In 1892, a merger of the Edison General Electric Company and the Thomson-Houston Electric Company created General Electric Company. GE is a diversified technology, manufacturing, and services company that operates in more than 100 countries around the world, with 250 manufacturing plants in 26 different nations. GE employs 276,000 people worldwide, including 165,000 in the United States. GE Plastics (GEP) is a world leader in versatile, high-performance engineered plastics used in the computer, electronics, office equipment, automotive, building and construction, and other industries.

With headquarters in Pittsfield, Massachusetts and technical facilities, manufacturing sites, and sales locations on five continents, GEP

Customer's color   Formula

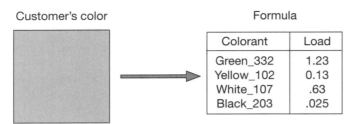

Colorant	Load
Green_332	1.23
Yellow_102	0.13
White_107	.63
Black_203	.025

Figure 4.1   Color matching input and output.

produces many of the world's best-known and most widely used polymers. Customers worldwide are served through regionally focused business centers led by our European headquarters in Bergen Op Zoom, The Netherlands, and in the Asia Pacific region at our Singapore headquarters.

4.2   The Problem

GE Plastics currently provides a color matching service to customers. Customers give GEP a physical sample of the color plastic they want, and GEP either finds a close match from their color library or formulates a new color to meet the customer's needs. (See Figure 4.1.) GEP currently has over 30,000 previously matched colors on file and performs approximately 4,000 color matches per year. Custom color matching and formula development is done at a significant cost to GEP, and the turnaround for the customer averages two weeks. The problem that we were trying to solve was how to reduce this cost and shorten the turnaround time.

4.2.1   The Existing Process

Selecting the colorants and loading levels for a color formula was previously accomplished by using a combination of human knowl-

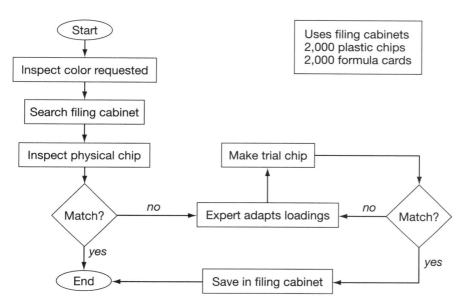

Figure 4.2 Old color matching process.

edge, working experience, and computationally expensive computer programs. Figure 4.2 shows the color matching process that was in place. The process starts with a skilled color matcher inspecting the color request for the type of plastic, the physical color standard supplied by the customer, and any special properties requested. The matcher then compares the customer's color standard with previous color chips that are stored in a filing cabinet. The filing cabinet holds about 2,000 plastic chips, approximately 2 by 3 by ⅛ inches, sorted by color.

The matcher selects the most similar color from the filing cabinet. Each chip is labeled, and another filing cabinet holds a formula card for each chip. The matcher then inspects the physical chip selected from the filing cabinet to determine if it matches the color and special properties requested by the customer. If it matches, the formula associated with the selected chip is used for the customer and the match is finished. If the best chip from the filing cabinet is not a satisfactory match, the matcher uses experience along with commercially available computer programs to adapt the colorant loadings.

The new loadings are used to create a small chip containing the adapted loadings. This chip is compared with the standard. If it is acceptable, the adapted formula is used for the customer and the chip is placed in the filing cabinet for future reference. If the color is unacceptable, the formula is adapted repeatedly until an acceptable formula is obtained.[1]

4.2.2 Background to Color Matching

There are commercially available computer programs that can calculate the colorant loading proportions for a color formula that matches a color standard. Since these programs perform an exhaustive search, they require users to select a subset of the allowable colorants. Usually five to seven are selected out of thirty to fifty possible colorants. The final formula will usually consist of four or five colorants. Having users make the critical decision of which colorants to select for the search often produces a less than optimal solution. Furthermore, it does not take into consideration other important attributes of a color match.

In order to convert a set of colorants and loadings into a single color, Kubelka-Munk theory can be used. This theory describes how the absorption and scattering of colorants in a material are related to its visible color. Each colorant contributes to the absorption and scattering of the material, and its contribution is proportional to the amount present in the system multiplied by an absorption and scattering coefficient for that colorant. The GEP system uses a modified Kubelka-Munk theory to characterize the relationship between pigment and dye concentrations with color.

---

1 This is an exceptionally clear example of the CBR methodology being used by people to solve a problem. This case study is using CBR to better manage a process that was already being done manually.

4.3 The Knowledge Management Solution

The approach taken was to create a software tool, called FormTool, that would automate and standardize the current color matching process and manage the knowledge involved in the process.

4.3.1 Expected Benefits

Automating the process with FormTool was expected to make color matching quicker and easier. Reducing the time needed to perform a color match would directly decrease the cost of the match and reduce the turnaround time. Making the color matching easier would allow less experienced matchers to perform a greater number of color matches and reduce problems caused by turnover in experienced color matchers. Further benefits could be achieved if the tool would allow the color matcher to perform a more thorough evaluation of the best formula, which would allow less expensive colorants to be used. Using low-cost colorants could provide a significant cost savings because the colorants are the most expensive component of plastic by weight, and the cost of different colorants can vary greatly.

4.3.2 The Team

GE has a research lab that works with all components of the company to introduce new technology or share existing technology. Bill Cheetham, who works at the research lab, supplied experience-creating tools that use information technology techniques, like case-based reasoning, to automate the existing processes. He worked with John Graf, a polymer scientist working at the component where the tool was to be used. John supplied the domain knowledge of color theory and worked on a daily basis with color matchers. It was important to have someone with experience creating tools and someone with domain knowledge on the project. Luckily, John is also a skilled programmer and was able to create a large part of the tool. Many of the color matchers were also involved in designing the user interface, determining the functionality that would be included, and testing early versions. Having the users give comments early in the development process was very helpful. Figure 4.3 shows John (right), Bill (center), and Dave Sorel (left), a color technician, in a color matching lab.

4.3.3 Implementation Plan

When the team started, they decided on a rapid prototyping development methodology, where working prototypes of increasing functionality would be created every few months. Before starting they identified the critical features, data sources, and user interface look and feel. The first prototype had the case base in the simplest possible format (a text file), a simple case selection technique (nearest neighbor), and a fairly nice user interface. The user interface was important for giving demonstrations to gain user feedback and management support. In

Figure 4.3   FormTool developers.

successive versions, new case base formats, selection techniques, adaptation techniques, and many useful features were created and evaluated. The best ones were kept and the old ones were discarded. For example, in the first prototype the speed of just the case selection was about four minutes. This decreased to about four seconds, including adaptation, in the current release.

4.3.4 Hardware and Software

The hardware selection was limited to the hardware that was currently available in the color matching lab. FormTool's hardware consists of a spectrophotometer attached to a personal computer running Windows 95. The spectrophotometer is used to determine a numerical representation of a color, called a reflectance curve. (See Figure 4.4.) The reflectance curve shows the percentage of light reflected by a material at each wavelength of the visible spectra (400nm to 700nm). A typical

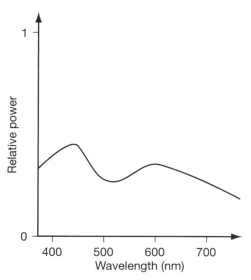

Figure 4.4 A Reflectance curve.

color spectrophotometer reads the reflectance of an object at 31 points equally spaced along the visible spectrum. Two spectra are compared by calculating the sum of squared differences, between two curves over all 31 points in the visible spectrum.

The software used to create FormTool required a little more evaluation. The team researched existing case-based reasoning tools, and the one that appeared to have the most promise was ART.[2] We created a quick prototype in ART, but found that ART (back in 1992) did not allow the flexibility of case selection needed. Furthermore, GE Plastics systems support would not be able to maintain an ART application after it was created. We needed to use tools that could be supported after FormTool was created. A custom development using a Visual Basic front end connected with C++ code for adaptation routines was selected. The case base was later stored in a Microsoft Access database.

4.3.5 System Architecture

The current process was already a case-based approach, where the filing cabinets acted as the case base and the color matcher searching through the filing cabinet was the case selection. Creating a tool to automate this involved creating a machine-readable version of the information in the filing cabinets and then creating the CBR software that performed the search. A numerical representation of the color of the plastic chips and their formulas was stored in a database that acted as the case-base. The automated color matching process is shown in Figure 4.5, which is just a modified version of Figure 4.2.

Figure 4.5 shows that the color matcher places the physical color standard in a spectrophotometer and reads the spectrum of the

---

2 The latest version of ART is marketed by MindBox. Their contact details can be found in the Appendix.

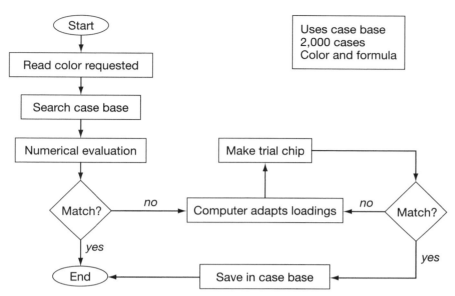

Figure 4.5 New color matching process.

color standard into the color matching system. Next, the color matcher enters key information such as the resin and grade of material in which to generate the match. FormTool then searches its case base of previous matches for the "best" previous match and adjusts those previous matches to produce a match for the new standard. The color match must satisfy multiple criteria: the color of the plastic must match the standard under multiple lighting conditions, there must be enough pigments to hide the color of the plastic, the cost of colorant formula should be as low as possible, only a limited amount of light can be transmitted through the plastic (optical density), and the color should not change when the plastic is molded at different temperatures.

The color matcher looks at the physical standard from this previous match and determines whether it is acceptable for the application and customer. If the match is not acceptable, FormTool adapts this previous match so that it more closely matches the requested color and application.[3] The color matcher then makes a physical chip using the adapted formula. If this new match is acceptable, the adapted loadings are saved into the database and the match is finished. If the match is not acceptable, the user can decide to do one of two things:

- manually or automatically adjust the color loadings, or
- switch to a different previous match as the starting point for this color match.

After one of these is done, the cycle continues until a match is found. The final match gives the "best" color match and balance of all other important properties.

4.3.6   Case Representation

The case base for the first version of FormTool used a text file. A later version used a binary file containing C data structures. A binary data structure was used as opposed to parsing a text file because it is easy and quick to load a case from a binary file. Each case in the case base contains a reflectance curve that represents the color matched, a list of pigments and loadings used to create that color, and some other general information. The data structure is shown in Figure 4.6. Later versions of FormTool used a Microsoft Access database to store the case base, but after the case selection was performed, the cases were placed in the same structure for analysis and adaptation.

4.3.7   Case Acquisition

The cases were obtained by combining information from two existing databases: a color standards database that stored the reflectance curve for

---

3 This is one of the few case studies in which the adaptation of the solution is performed automatically by the computer program. This is possible in this example because the adaptation can be done using explicit knowledge coded as mathematical formulas. Nonetheless, if adaptation is not successful, human input is required.

```
typedef struct CaseInfo_Struct{
   short int caseNumber;            /*unique number for case */
   char colorID[20];               /*unique human readable ID for case */
   float spectra[32];              /*numerical desciption of color*/
   char spectroStatus[20];         /*status of machine while reading
                                     spectra
*/
   char resin[20];                 /*the type of plastic used for match*/
   char grade[20];                 /*the subtype of plastic */
   char date[20];                  /*date of color match*/
   char site[20];                  /*location color match was performed
   */
   float numPigments;              /*number of pigments in match */
   struct aPigment pigments[15];   /*names & amounts of pigments used*/
}CaseInfo;
```

Figure 4.6   Case representation.

all colors used in production and a BOM (bill of materials) database that stored all formulas. The color ID, resin, and grade were needed to uniquely identify a color match and were stored in both databases. We combined the information from the two databases to create the case base.

As part of creating the case base it needed to be checked for accuracy and coverage. Some of the data from the databases was not correct, so we wanted to remove any bad cases that were created from incorrect data. We also wanted to make sure that we had previous matches for all colors that we would want to match in the future. We used two methods for checking the accuracy: an algorithm that predicted the color from the formula and data mining for trends in the data that could be consistent errors. It was impossible to make an algorithm that was very accurate in predicting the color, but an algorithm could still point out the cases that were drastically incorrect. We used the algorithm to point out cases where the color did not match the formula within a set threshold and then evaluated all of the cases with a large error by hand.

The data mining technique that worked best for finding erroneous cases was a graphing tool. Figure 4.7 shows the initial case base, where the difference in the color predicted by the formula and the color, dl, is

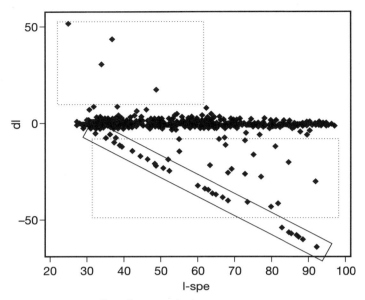

Figure 4.7   Case-base analysis.

plotted against the color spectra, l-spe. The graph shows a diagonal box with matches that had their color spectra entered incorrectly. The other two boxes contain matches where the formula and color spectra were not matched together correctly. The matches in the three boxes represented only 4 percent of the case base, so we removed all these matches.

Checking the case base for coverage was done by plotting the case base on a two-dimensional view of color space, then checking that there is coverage throughout color space. We found that there were many gray matches and not very many bright reds or yellows. Because of this we removed some overlapping gray matches and attempted to get more brightly colored matches. However, we found that GE does not do many brightly colored matches. To accommodate bright color matches when there is no existing color match, we created an alternative method of producing a color match that is not as accurate as the

CBR approach, but can be used when there is no existing case close to the desired color.[4]

4.3.8   Case Retrieval

This section describes a method to evaluate the quality of a specific color formula. A selection process that uses this method to evaluate a formula can be used to find the formula that will reproduce a specified color and meet all desired attributes for the application of the specified color. Nearest neighbor retrieval is used. However, the nearest neighbor must be determined by evaluating the degree of match in all of the attributes described earlier. This evaluation needs to provide a consistent meaning of an attribute's similarity throughout all attributes. The consistency is achieved through the use of fuzzy linguistic terms, such as Excellent, Good, Fair, and Poor, which are associated with measured differences in an attribute. Any number of linguistic terms can be used. A fuzzy preference function is used to calculate the similarity of a single attribute of a case with the corresponding attribute of the subject. (See Figure 4.8.)

In Figure 4.8, a difference of 1 unit in the values of that attribute for the subject and comparable would be considered excellent, a difference of 2 would be good, 3 would be fair, and 4 would be poor. This rating is then transformed into the fuzzy preference function in Figure 4.8.

The result of using fuzzy preference functions is a vector, called the fuzzy preference vector. The vector contains a fuzzy preference value for each attribute. The values in this vector can be combined, through weighted aggregation, to produce a robust similarity value. The use of fuzzy preference functions allows for smooth changes in the result

---

4 Although case data existed, it is normal for developers of a CBR system to have to preprocess the existing data. The team here has been particularly thorough and methodical in their approach and has cleaned the data as well as removing redundant cases and checking that there is an even spread (coverage) of cases across the problem space.

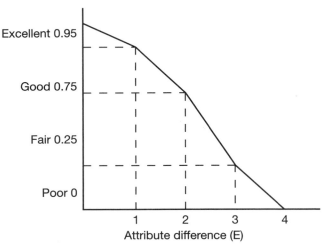

Figure 4.8   Fuzzy preference function.

when an attribute is changed, unlike the large changes that are possible when step functions are used.

A fuzzy preference function is used to transform a quantifiable value for each attribute into a qualitative description of the attribute that can be compared with the qualitative description of other attributes. A fuzzy preference function allows a comparison of properties that are based on entirely different scales, such as cost measured in cents per pound and spectral curve match measured in reflection units. Based on discussions with experts and work to classify previous matches into various sets of linguistic terms, we found that there was enough precision in our evaluation of the similarity of the attributes to have four linguistic terms. Table 4.1 shows the linguistic terms and the numeric similarity score that corresponds to each term.

Fuzzy preference functions were created for each of the following attributes of the color match:

■ color similarity,
■ total colorant load,
■ cost of colorant formula,

Table 4.1   Global preference function scale.

Fuzzy Rating	Maximum Score	Maximum Score
Excellent	1	0.95
Good	0.94	0.75
Average	0.74	0.25
Poor	0.24	0

■ optical density of color, and
■ color shift when molded under normal and abusive conditions.

The remainder of this section describes how the fuzzy preference functions were constructed for each attribute.

Color Similarity

Two different ways of rating the quality of a color match are the spectral color curve match and metamerism of the color. Matching the spectral curve is the best way to match a color for all possible lighting conditions. Minimizing metamerism, which reduces the color difference under the most common lighting conditions, is the traditional way a color match was done before there was a spectrophotometer that could read the reflectance of a color. Both of these methods are useful in matching a color.

The spectral color curve match is a rating of how closely the color of the formula created matches the color of the standard. A spectral curve is a representation of the amount of light that is reflected from an object at each wavelength of the visible spectrum. Comparing spectral curves of objects is the best way to compare their color, because if the two objects have the same spectral curve, their colors will match under all lighting conditions. Other color matching techniques only match colors under one lighting condition, so the colors can look quite different under other lighting conditions.

Table 4.2 Match quality rating.

Fuzzy Rating	Maximum Sum of Squares Difference
Excellent	0.000124
Good	0.000496
Fair	0.001984
Poor	0.007936

The spectral curve match is characterized by the sums of the squared differences in the reflection values at 31 wavelengths from 400nm to 700nm at a 10nm interval. Table 4.2 shows the value of that sum of squares that is needed for an Excellent, Good, Fair, or Poor match. These values are determined by having a subject matter expert rate the curve matches in the case base and then finding the minimum value for each of the ratings, excluding a few outliers.

For example, a sum of square difference of 0.000124 is the maximum difference for an excellent rating, from Table 4.2. The score corresponding to this would be 0.95, the minimum score for "Excellent" from Table 4.2. Sum of square values between the minimum and maximum values have scores that are linearly interpolated from the minimum and maximum values for that rating.

Total Loading

The total colorant load is the total volume of all colorants used for a set volume of plastic. It is best to use the least volume of colorants that makes an acceptable match, for reasons relating to the manufacturing of the plastic.

The quality of the remaining properties depends on the color that is being matched. For example, a cost that is good for a red color might be poor for a white because reds are much more expensive. In order to use fuzzy preference functions for these attributes, the case base must be subdivided into portions that have consistent values for the properties. We have divided the case base into eleven classes. Figure

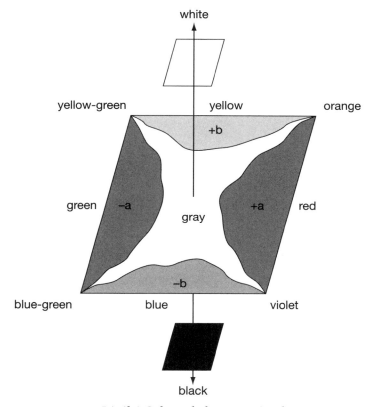

Figure 4.9 L*a*b* Color subclasses retrieval.

4.9 lists those classes and shows where they are in the L*a*b* color space. For each attribute, the fuzzy ratings needed to be calculated separately for each subclass.

An attribute that uses these subclasses is the total loading of colorant in the formula. The total colorant loading of the formula can be characterized in parts per hundred (pph) of base material such as plastic. The total colorant loading depends on the color to be made. Table 4.3 shows the fuzzy ratings for total colorant loading for the white and green color subclasses. The rest of the subclasses are similar to the ones presented. Historically, whites tend to require much more colorant

Table 4.3 Fuzzy measure for total colorant loading.

Fuzzy Rating	White pph	Green pph
Excellent	3	0.4
Good	5	0.7
Fair	7	1.1
Poor	11	3.2

Table 4.4 Fuzzy measure for cost.

Fuzzy Rating	Red Cost (cents/lb)	Blue Cost (cents/lb)
Excellent	4.5	2
Good	9	3.5
Fair	25	10
Poor	72	28

than a green color. This is because it takes more of the white colorant to hide the color of the plastic. The difference in typical loadings is accounted for by using separate tables for separate colors. A fuzzy preference function can be easily constructed for each subclass.

Cost

The cost of the colorants in the formula should be kept to a minimum to maximize the profitability of the manufacturing process.

The cost attribute is measured in units of cents per pound. The fuzzy ratings for this attribute are specific for particular color subclasses, as illustrated for the red and blue subclasses in Table 4.4. The mapping differs for the red and blue color families because the cost of colorants to make a red tend to be more expensive than the colorants used to make a blue.

Table 4.5   Fuzzy measure for optical density.

Fuzzy Rating	Grey dE*	Red dE*
Excellent	5.9	5.9
Good	5.8	5
Fair	5.5	2
Poor	4	1

Optical Density

The *optical density* of plastic is the thickness of plastic that is required to stop all light from radiating through the plastic. A specific optical density is required for many applications. For the majority of color formulas, it is desirable to make the material opaque to prevent light from transmitting through the material. Optical density can be used to characterize how much light is transmitted through a sample. The type of colorants used in a formula and the loading level of the colorants determine the optical density of the material. The qualitative values of optical density are color dependent. For example, it is easier to obtain the needed optical density in an opaque gray color formula than in a red color. Table 4.5 shows the fuzzy rating of optical density for a gray and a red color.

Hide Color Shift

The color shift when molding under normal and abusive conditions comes from the fact that the plastic can be molded at low and high temperatures. The same plastic is a slightly different color when molded at different temperatures, because plastic tends to yellow at higher temperatures. In order to minimize the color shift, extra colorant loadings need to be used. A formula must also be robust enough to hide these color changes in the base plastic. One way to characterize this attribute of hiding variations due to process conditions is to measure the color of the material under normal processing conditions and

Table 4.6   Fuzzy measure for color shift.

Fuzzy Rating	Grey dE*	Yellow dE*
Excellent	0.05	0.05
Good	0.10	0.15
Fair	0.2	0.4
Poor	0.5	1.0

under abusive processing conditions. The difference in color between these two processing conditions is then measured in dE* units using the CIE L*a*b* color scale. Table 4.6 shows the process color change in dE* units mapped between the gray and yellow color subclasses. Visually, a larger change in color due to processing conditions can be tolerated in a light yellow color than a gray color, as shown by this mapping based on historical data.

Aggregate Fuzzy Preference Values

Each of the properties discussed so far, including spectral color match, metameric index, loading level, cost, optical density, and color shift due to processing conditions, is based on different scales of units. By mapping each of these properties to a global scale through the use of fuzzy preferences and linguistic terms such as Excellent, Good, Fair, and Poor, it becomes possible to compare one attribute with another.

The next step is to create a summation of the preference value of each attribute. This can be done with a weight of unity for each attribute, or end users can supply weights of their own if they wish to emphasize one attribute over another. Dividing this summation term by the summation of the weights gives the global preference value for the system.

4.3.9   Case Adaptation

Most formulas that are retrieved need some adaptation. The similarity calculation described above is used to guide the adaptation. Adaptation is done by performing a search. The search repeatedly varies the load-

Table 4.7   Colorant types and colorants.

Colorant Types	Colorants of that Colorant Type
White	Ivory, Pure, Bright
Black	Coal, Midnight
Red	Crimson, Garnet, Wine, Fire, Maroon
Orange	Orange, Pumpkin
Yellow	Canary, Lemon, Sunflower

ings of the colorants in the formula retrieved and evaluates the new similarity. Kubelka-Munk theory is used as part of the similarity calculation and provides a formula for predicting the color change from modifying the loadings of the colorants. Having a function that can accurately evaluate the effect of an adaptation is the key to performing the correct adaptation.[5]

4.3.10   Alternative Method of Color Matching

If case-based reasoning does not produce a solution, an alternative method of searching for an acceptable match can be used. This alternative method uses trends from the case base to guide a search of all possible solutions. This section will show how a search can be guided by statistics from the case base. Before the trends were calculated, the colorants were clustered into colorant types and each previous case was classified as a specific color class (red, blue, etc.). The colorants were classified such that each colorant type contains a list of all colorants that are considered to belong to that type. (See Table 4.7.) For example, the colorant type White contains three colorants: Ivory, Pure,

---

5 This is an unusual example where explicit formalized knowledge is available to automate the case revision or adaptation process. It shows that when this knowledge is available the process within the CBR-cycle can be successfully automated. However, as the other case studies show, it is rare for this knowledge to be available.

and Bright. These are all of the white colorants. Each colorant is a member of at least one colorant type, but a colorant could be in more than one colorant type (for example, a greenish blue could be in the colorant types Green and Blue).

Table 4.8 shows five of the color classes and the number of previous cases that belong to each of those classes. Now that the colorant types and color classes have been constructed, we can calculate trends for each color class. Trends for a color class are much more informative than trends for the entire case base.

For each color class (red, blue, etc.) there are certain combinations of colorant types that have been used more often in the past. Table 4.9 shows the combinations, called keys, for making red colors. The most common key is to use three colorants, one each from the colorant types white, black, and red. Color matches for color standards that were classified as red used colorants from these three colorant types

Table 4.8   Color classes retrieval.

Color Class	Number of Cases in that Color Class
White	560
Black	439
Red	273
Orange	255
Yellow	212
Total =	1739

Table 4.9   Formula keys for making red color matches retrieval.

Formula Keys	Colorants for Each Key	% Using Key
Key 1	White + Black + Red	23
Key 2	White + Black + Red + Yellow	19
Key 3	White + Black + Red + Yellow + Orange	15
Key 4	White + Black + Red + Orange	14

23 percent of the time. When creating a color match for a new color that is classified as red, it is likely that the colorants used will belong to one of the keys that were created for the color red. Figure 4.10 shows a process for generating all of the combinations of colorants that are possible for all keys of a color class. The color standard that the customer submitted for a color match is classified as a color class. Then, all keys for that color class are retrieved from a database of keys. The first key is used to generate all combinations of colorants that match the key. Table 4.10 shows all sets of colorants that match the first red key. The best match can be saved, or if one of these matches is good enough (it meets all criteria specified by a user), the process can be stopped. After all combinations for one key are tried, the next key will be used to generate all combinations possible for it. After all keys have been used, the process will end. The best match that was saved during the search will be displayed to a user.

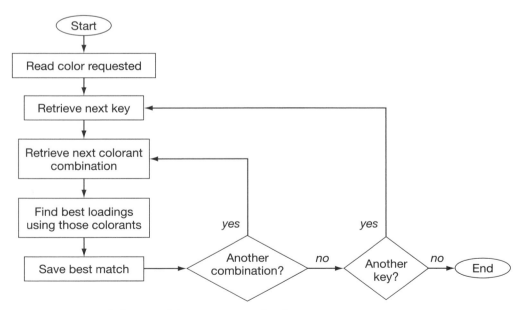

Figure 4.10   Color matching process retrieval.

Table 4.10   Colorant sets that match the first key.

Colorant Combinations

1. Ivory + Coal + Crimson
2. Ivory + Coal + Garnet
3. Ivory + Coal + Wine
4. Ivory + Coal + Fire
5. Ivory + Coal + Maroon
6. Ivory + Midnight + Crimson
. . .
30. Bright + Midnight + Maroon

4.3.11   Case Retention

Case retention is done automatically. Whenever a color match is saved, the case is automatically submitted to the case base. However, a script is automatically run on the new candidate case to check if a similar case is already in the case base. If there is no similar case, the new match is added to the case base. The script does not add the case if it is similar so that we do not swamp the case base with too many similar matches.[6]

4.3.12   Interface Design

The interface was designed at the start of the project. Paper versions of the interface were created with the color matchers. We also collected the items that were critical to the quality (CTQs) of the tool. Some of these CTQs were:

- A simple user interface with everything on one screen
- A color match that worked in all lighting conditions and also met other customer requirements

---

6 The review process of the CBR-cycle has therefore been automated in this system.

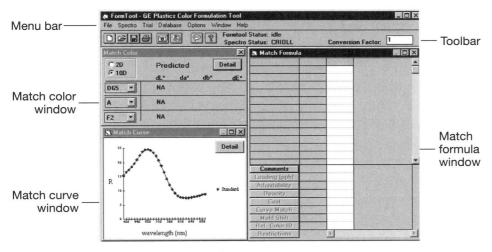

Figure 4.11   FormTool main windows.

- The lowest-cost color match
- A color match that is easy to manufacture

Then a prototype was created. The color matchers evaluated the prototype, and they came up with other items that were critical for the tool to have:

- Ability to see multiple (five) previous color matches
- Ability to manually change and evaluate a selected match
- Ability to see what the previous match was before it was adapted
- An alternate method of creating a match if no previous similar matches existed

These items were added and a production version was created. One of the first production versions is shown in Figure 4.11.

FormTool's main display consists of a menu bar and toolbar, which are always located at the top of the screen, plus three other windows (Match Color, Match Curve, and Match Formula), which can be moved and resized in the bottom portion of the display. The menu bar and toolbar are used to enter various commands.

The Match Color window, on the upper left, shows the dL*, da*, db*, and dE* of the current trial compared with the standard. The current trial is the trial in the leftmost (gray) position in the Match Formula window. The deltas are calculated under three different lighting conditions. A wide range of lighting conditions can be specified. A different lighting condition can be selected by clicking on the down arrow on the combo box on the left side of the window. The radio boxes set the standard observer as either 2 degree or 10 degree. If the spectra for the physical chip for a trial has not been read, the values shown are the differences between the predicted spectra and the standard spectra. The predicted dL*, da*, db*, and dE* are calculated knowing the colorant's loading, scattering, and absorption. If the predicted spectrum is used, the word "Predicted" is displayed at the top of the Match Color window. If the physical trial has been read, the differences between the physical trial and physical standard are displayed. In this case, the phrase "Trial Chip" is displayed at the top of the Match Color window.

The Match Curve window, in the lower left, displays the spectral curve from 400nm to 700nm for the following spectra:

- *Standard.* The standard spectrum read in with the spectrophotometer
- *Predicted.* The spectrum that is calculated from absorption and scattering of the colorants
- *Actual trial.* The results of a trial batch as read with a spectrophotometer

The standard spectrum is graphed if the physical standard has been read. The predicted spectrum is graphed if a predicted formula exists. The trial spectrum is graphed if the physical chip for the current trial has been read.

The Match Formula window, on the right, displays the colorants and loadings for every trial and various attributes of each trial. In the top half, the colorant names are given in the leftmost column. Every other column is a different trial at matching the standard. Trials can be moved or deleted by using the Trial menu items, Select Current Trial and Delete Trial. The trial in the leftmost column is the current trial. The Match Color, Match Curve, and all the detail windows describe the current trial. You can also double-click on the column of a trial to make it the current trial (the trial gets moved to the leftmost column). In the bottom half, the results of a match evaluation are displayed for each trial.

The three windows show the basic information needed to perform a color match. More detailed information can be obtained from each window. The Match Color and Match Curve windows each have a button labeled Detail to obtain the detailed description. For the Match Formula window, a button describing each attribute (adjustability, opacity, cost, etc.) can be clicked with the mouse to present a window with further detail on that particular attribute.

The three windows can be resized (by clicking and dragging on the left, right, and bottom borders of the window), moved (by clicking and dragging on the top border), or hidden (by clicking on the minimize button in the top right corner of each window) so that users can format the main windows to their liking.

4.3.13   Testing

The system was tested in several ways:

- The case base was tested as described previously.
- Multiple case selection algorithms were tested and compared on a case base with 1700 cases.
- The adaptation algorithms were tested and validated against experimental data.
- The entire system was tested on 100 previous matches.
- Finally, at each location where the system was used, it was tested side-by-side with the previous methods of color matching, and the

results were compared. In each location the case-based approach was found to produce superior results.

4.3.14 Rollout

FormTool was originally developed and paid for by GE Plastics' Cycolac business located at Parkersburg, West Virginia. After it was shown that the project costs were recovered within the first six months of operation of the software, other GE Plastic product business leaders became interested in the tool. The first challenge in rolling out the software to all GE Plastic color matching labs was to make the tool and database capable of handling the diverse range of products and types of colors that GE made. For example, the Cycolac product line doesn't make transparent or translucent colors, but the Lexan product line does. So algorithms had to be modified to handle these new color types to make the tool product-line generic.

Although these technical challenges were complex, they were easy compared to the organizational issues that caused the rollout to be neither smooth nor fast. The color matching operation within GE Plastics in 1996 was decentralized over ten different labs falling under different profit/loss centers around the world. Rollout issues included language differences (Japanese, French, Italian, Korean, and Chinese) and resistance to making the necessary process changes to implement the software tool. Each site required us to run experiments proving that the FormTool software was better than their current process due to the "our product and process is different" theme that we encountered at each facility. In the end it was GE Plastics' decision to make an organizational change and consolidate the color match labs that led to the use of the FormTool software across all the product-line businesses.

4.4 System Demonstration

This section will describe how a color technician uses the FormTool software to generate a color match.

4.4.1 Enter Color Match Request Input

The process begins when the color technician has all the input information, including:

- The physical color sample to match, which can be of any type (such as a plastic chip, paper, cloth, ceramic, string, or numerical readings)
- The type of resin (Cycolac, Lexan, Noryl, etc.) and grade of material (GPM5600, C1950, 121, etc.) to use for creating the match
- Application requirements such as FDA approval (food grade), light sources, and opacity

This is the minimum amount of information necessary to begin a CMR (Color Match Request). Each CMR is given a unique number for tracking, and all of the CMR information is entered into the FormTool software by completing a two-page form, one page of which is shown in Figure 4.12.

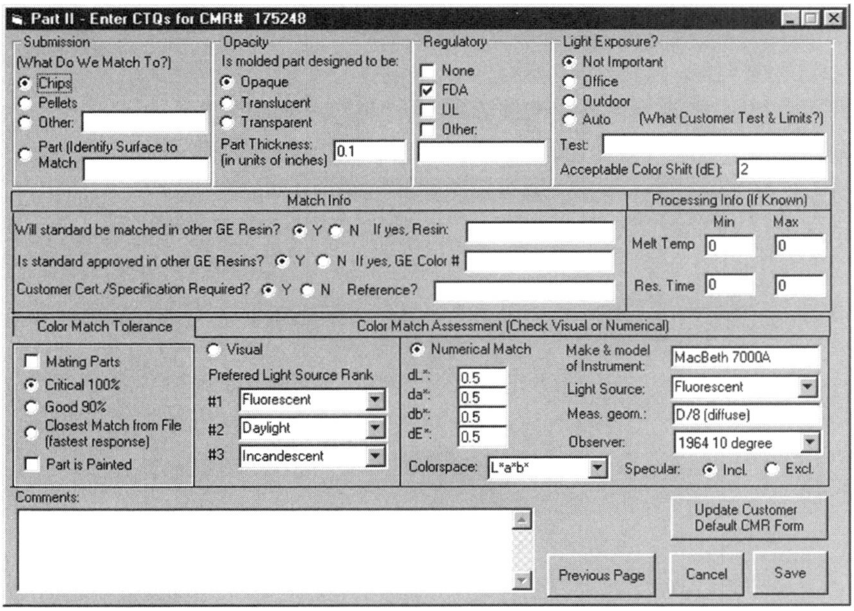

Figure 4.12 Color match requirements.

The technician (color matcher) then places the physical color standard, supplied by the customer, into the spectrophotometer. FormTool controls the spectrophotometer and reads the spectrum of the request. The spectral information is saved along with other key information (such as the resin and grade of the material) requested by the customer.

4.4.2 Perform Color Match Case-Base Research

Once the input for a color match is entered and saved into the FormTool system, the technician selects the Do Case Base Research menu command. This command begins the case base selection process, followed by case adaptation, with the results displayed to the user. The main screens of the FormTool software will be updated to show the match. Figure 4.13 shows the suggested trial colorants and the absolute colorant loadings in parts per hundred (pph) resin. The Set Conversion Factor menu item in the Options menu allows the user to scale the formula to any batch size (for example, 1354 grams per batch). The Match Curve window shows both the standard spectra and

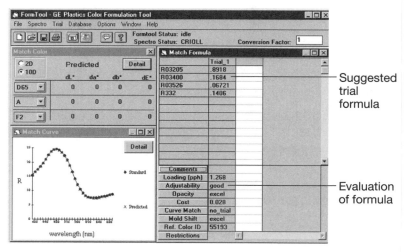

Figure 4.13 Main screens with suggested trial.

the predicted trial spectra, and the Match Color window shows the predicted dL*, da*, db*, and dE* values, which show how closely the colors match.

The bottom half of the Match Formula window presents the total loading of colorant, the adjustability, opacity, cost, and so on. Greater detail for each of these items can be obtained by clicking the mouse on the description buttons.

4.4.3 Experimentally Validate Adapted Case

When the technician is satisfied that the predicted formula suggested will yield the best match for the request (based on comparing the spectra produced by reading the customer's request with the predicted spectra of the trial formula), the formula can be submitted for weigh-up. A trial chip is manufactured, and this physical trial is then read into the same CMR. This reading of the trial allows FormTool to generate mathematical and graphical comparisons of the customer's request with the trial plaque.

4.4.4 Determine Whether Match Is Acceptable

At this point a decision has to be made to determine whether the spectral curves and visual match are good enough, for the customer and application. If the trial is good enough, the match is finished. If the trial does not give a good enough match, the user should adjust the relative ratios of the trial using a statistical function called Color Correction. If the initial formula does not look like it will ever produce an acceptable match, another initial match can be obtained by evaluating the next best suggestion resulting from the case base process.

4.5 Maintenance

The FormTool case base currently resides in a Microsoft Access database format and requires minimal maintenance. The main responsibility of the database administrator assigned to the database is data security and data backup. There is an effort under way to convert the case base from a Microsoft Access format to Oracle to make this job easier, since Oracle is the standard for General Electric.

New cases are automatically added to the database each time a color match is performed and saved. Filtering algorithms are run just before adding a new case to make sure it is nonredundant. This has made it possible to keep the case base optimized as it grows with time.

Functionality built into the software allows color specialists to add new pigments and dyes to the tool. This process involves producing a number of color batches used to characterize the optical properties of the pigment or dye that are then saved in the tool to be used in the case-adaptation algorithms. Additionally, the color specialist is responsible for entering the rules for each pigment or dye. These rules include which product grade the pigment can be used in and at what minimum and maximum concentrations. Since new pigments or dyes are added infrequently, this does not consume much time.

4.6 Benefits[7]

GE Plastics has obtained significant savings in both time and money by using the FormTool software for color matching since the beginning of 1995. The hard savings that have been documented come from the optimization of pigment and dye concentrations and the reduction in the number of trial batches required for a color match. When the tool was first rolled out at the end of 1994, the optimization algorithms for pig-

---

7 The authors have recently published a paper detailing the benefits of their system in more detail: Cheetham, W. (2001). "Benefits of Case-Based Reasoning in Color Matching." In *Case-Based Reasoning Research & Develpment,* Springer, LNAI 2080, pp. 589–596.

ment and dye concentrations were run against the historical database of formulas, resulting in the identification of formulas that could have their colorant concentrations reduced while maintaining the quality of the color match. These changes led to a reduction in the raw material cost of the final product, generating significant cost reductions to the company. The reduction in the number of trial batches required to obtain a color match has led GEP to cut its turnaround time for a custom color match from an average of two weeks to forty-eight hours.

The average number of test chips created per color match has decreased from 4.2 to 2.7. This is an average reduction of 4.5 hours per color match. Since over 5,000 matches are performed per year, this saves 22,500 hours. The custom color match is a free service to customers, so a reasonable estimate of the direct cost saving is $2.25 million per year. We also estimate a saving in pigment costs of a further $2.4 million per year.

A number of other benefits have been harder to quantify. Each factory that has implemented the software needed to standardize their process of color matching before they could take advantage of the software. Through managing this knowledge explicitly, the quality of the color match from the various GEP factories has improved and become more consistent across the world. Additionally, the ability to share data and knowledge across the sites has resulted in greater case base growth, leading to greater sharing of color matching experience and knowledge. When FormTool was first used in 1995 the case base contained 1,700 records. At the end of 1997 the case base had grown to over 20,000 records. FormTool is now used for approximately 4,000 color matches per year and is expected to grow as more European and Asian factories implement FormTool.

The U.S. Patent and Trademark office has granted GE four patents on various aspects of the color matching process described here. A European patent has also been filed.

■ Patent No. 5,668,633; Method and System for Formulating a Color Match

- Patent No. 5,720,017; System and Method for Formulating a Color Match Using Color Keys
- Patent No. 5,740,078; Method and System for Determining Optimum Colorant Loading Using Merit Functions
- Patent No. 5,841,421; Method and System for Selecting a Previous Color Match from a Set of Previous Matches

4.7 Conclusion

The FormTool software has been considered a success at General Electric due to the project's financial return on investment. It is also considered a technology achievement due to the number of patents obtained and the opportunities it has opened up. ColorXpress Select is a new online tool (located at http://www.gecolorxpress.com) that allows registered users to access GE's color match library. This Java tool developed by the GE Corporate Research & Development Center allows color match cases to be selected over the Web. Instead of performing a case selection within GE Plastics by color technicians, customers can perform their own selection process.

GEP is currently working on two new CBR knowledge management tools. The first system allows customers to select the appropriate type of plastic to meet their engineering requirements. The second system will help GE researchers develop new plastics by providing a common repository for sharing knowledge about experiments and designing new experiments.

Improving Process Design

Knowledge Sharing in Aluminum Foundries

Chris Price
Centre for Intelligent Systems
University of Wales

5.1 Introduction

This chapter describes a knowledge management system that troubleshoots the manufacturing process in aluminum die-casting foundries in the U.K. Established in 1974, Wilson & Royston Ltd. has subsidiaries in the U.K., U.S., Spain, and Mexico. They combine their manufacturing experience with state-of-the-art technology and integrated CAD/CAM to provide a specialist service for pressure die-casting tools, plastic and rubber injection, compression and transfer moulds, jigs, fixtures, and press tools, plus a precision machining service.

The accumulation of past knowledge is a by-product of the normal working practice of reporting problems within a foundry, rather than by the creation of a new software maintenance action. Solutions to past problems are stored as cases, and CBR finds possible solutions when new problems occur. A significant advancement in the use of CBR for troubleshooting applications is that cases become a resource for improving process design by reducing the incidence of similar problems in the future.

5.2 The Problem

Two kinds of primary processes are used within aluminum die-casting:

- Gravity die-casting, where molten metal is poured into a die, or mould. This is useful for casting relatively simple shapes when a low volume of parts is required.
- Pressure die-casting, where molten metal is injected at high pressure into the die. This is the more common technique for mass-producing a large number of parts, or when more complex shapes are required.

Customers expect die-casters to produce finished or near-finished parts; so in practice foundries perform a number of secondary operations in addition to die-casting. There are also several operations carried out prior to the casting stage. For this reason the term *die-casting* in this chapter is used in the broader sense, to mean the production of finished (or near-finished) parts from raw materials; in other words, *all* the stages involved in the manufacturing process (drilling, lathing, painting, etc.), not just the act of pouring molten metal or injecting it into a die.

Several problems are associated with die-casting:

- Typically, the customer is responsible for the design of the part and often has little or no regard for the processes employed to produce it. That is, functional considerations take precedence over production considerations. In addition, the customer has aesthetic considerations that can sometimes place unnecessary constraints on the die-caster. Quality expectations can also be unrealistically high due to insufficient in-depth knowledge of the processes used in die-casting.

■ Keeping track of problems can be difficult. Failures discovered at late stages of manufacture are often caused by early manufacturing stages. Moreover, certain problems tend to reoccur less frequently than others, making it difficult to find out how a failure was dealt with on a previous occasion. Experienced foundry staff tend to fix problems without needing to refer to past records, but when key staff retire or change jobs, this knowledge is lost.

■ Tracing the root causes of quality-related problems can also be difficult. Foundry staff rely on experience when deciding on which paths to investigate, because looking at all the possibilities would be impractical or too time consuming.

Two paper-based systems were in use at the foundries: Process Concern Reports (PCR) and Eight Discipline (8D) reports.[1] Both of these systems were used for reporting foundry problems. When a problem with a part was reported, either by a customer or from within the foundry, a new PCR would be raised. The form records all the information concerning the problem, customer details, the actions to remedy the problem, and a list of personnel carrying out the recommended actions. The form is then circulated among the personnel named on the form, the actions are carried out, and the PCR closed once the problem is solved. Once closed, the PCR is filed for later reference.

This type of system is valuable because it is a record of the foundry's troubleshooting experience. The quantity of paper involved, however, made it impractical to search and retrieve appropriate records for problem-solving purposes.

---

1 The 8D methodology was also used by National Semiconductor in the first case study.

5.3 The Knowledge Management Solution

Certain types of problems are common enough for foundry staff to know what to do without having to refer to any kind of records or documentation. Less common failures are more likely to be problematic because the experience gained from fixing such a problem on a previous occasion is more likely to be lost. Even if the information was recorded, finding the appropriate records when required can prove difficult, especially with paper-based systems. This makes CBR an obvious knowledge management methodology to use.

Very often paper-based records already exist, which make good raw material for case-based systems. It is just a question of identifying them and storing them in an accessible way. The PCR and 8D reports were used as the basis for a computer system that records problems in a case base used as a resource for troubleshooting by employing CBR techniques.

5.3.1 Expected Benefits

Predicting the benefits from the implementation of a knowledge management system is rarely straightforward. Process improvements and intangible efficiency gains are not always easy to quantify. Thus, it is helpful to look for a quantifiable measure that may approximate obtainable benefits. In an aluminum foundry a reduction in the amount of scrap metal generated, mostly caused by failed castings, is one such metric. At the beginning of this project we estimated that the combined use of the systems would realize a 10 percent reduction of scrap metal. This in turn would save an estimated $150,000 a year at each foundry.

5.3.2 The Team

This project, called QPAC,[2] was a three-year research project involving the University of Wales at Aberystwyth and three aluminum die-

2 Further details on the project, including software downloads, are available from the Web at http://users.aber.ac.uk/cjp/QPACweb/.

casters, namely Kaye (Presteigne) Ltd., Burdon and Miles Ltd., and Morris Ashby Castings, all owned by Wilson & Royston. The main aims of the project were as follows:

- Capture of information relating to foundry problems
- Reuse of this information for troubleshooting foundry-related problems and for providing statistical information
- Automation of Process Failure Modes and Effects Analysis (Process FMEA)

5.3.3   Implementation Plan

Our approach was to develop integrated software tools that can share information stored in databases. Real data had to be used to test our software. This means building tools robust enough to be tested and used in real industrial environments. To this end, prototype software tools have been delivered to our industrial collaborators during the course of the project. They have been used in each foundry over some years.

Each foundry has a network of PCs and servers. The existing systems used at each of the sites were very similar. Because the aim of the project was to develop tools that could perform different tasks but share data and knowledge, we used conventional databases to store information. We wanted to gather realistic data quickly. To this end, we used Delphi as our software development tool. This enabled us to deliver prototypes quickly and gather information and feedback from our industrial partners.

The main CBR tool is the PCR system, which records foundry problems and uses its database as a case-base for troubleshooting. The Statistical Process Control (SPC) system records results of SPC studies and uses CBR to predict process capability. The Process Flowchart system is used to design the complete casting process. The result of this design is a list of processes, which forms the framework for the auto-generation of Process Failure Modes Effect Analysis (FMEA).

Both the SPC and PCR systems are referenced during FMEA generation. The SPC system provides useful information for finding the occurrence of certain problems. References to real PCRs are used in the FMEA so that the generic results the system generates can be compared with real-life problems.

5.3.4 System Architecture

As previously mentioned, two paper-based systems held valuable troubleshooting information, namely, the PCR and 8D reports. We decided to build a database system that would combine the information stored in these two reports. In order to gather as much realistic data as possible, this system was implemented at the earliest possible stage, and has now replaced the paper-based systems at all three foundries. The PCR system is now on the foundries' networks so that users can access the system from any terminal.

The automated PCR system has four main functions:

1. To hold information for PCR and 8D reports
2. To facilitate troubleshooting by employing CBR techniques
3. To provide graphical information on problems within the foundry
4. To provide a source of information for automating Process FMEA

The PCR system is a source of past cases of problems with solutions. Given a current PCR as input, the system looks through the list of completed PCRs for the ones that it deems to be the most similar. The solutions from the chosen past cases may then give valuable information on how to solve the current problem. The CBR system uses the nearest neighbor method for retrieving cases. A schematic of the system architecture is shown in Figure 5.1.

The Process Flowchart System
One part of IS0-9000 (APQP—Advanced Product Quality Planning) requires the drawing of a flowchart that represents the sequence of steps involved in the production of a particular manufactured product.

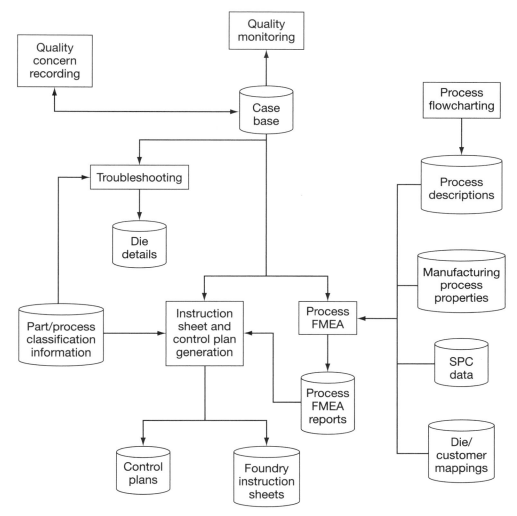

Figure 5.1   System Architecture.

The production of this flowchart involves a certain amount of input from the customer; so there is inevitably some faxing or emailing back and forth of prototype charts before both sides are happy with the result. The flowchart is graphical in nature and employs a set of symbols to denote specific types of process.

The flowchart system produced by QPAC employs the same conventions as the manual system already in use at Morris Ashby's. Flowcharts are stored in a database and can be printed graphically from within the program. The use of symbols (and optionally color) makes it easier to spot weaknesses in the process sequence (such as a run of operations with no inspection stages). (See Figure 5.2.)

The process names used by the flowchart system are the same as those employed by the PCR system. A database table specifies all the allowable failure modes for each process recognized by the system, while a separate maintenance system allows the user to alter the tables. Having the same names for processes and failures in all systems helps the automation of Process FMEA. The FMEA system, which is incorporated into the process-flowchart program, takes the list of processes from the appropriate flowchart and, using the process/failure table, generates all the combinations of processes and failures required for a Process FMEA. Each line of the FMEA has a list of PCRs associated with it (for example, completed PCRs that match the process, failure, and part category). Accessing the SPC system (described next) can also generate certain values required for Process FMEA.

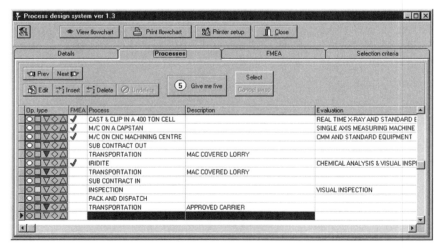

Figure 5.2 The Process Design system showing the main flowchart information.

The SPC System

The Statistical Process Control system is a database for recording the results of SPC studies (that is, Process Capability studies and Machine Capability studies). It includes a feature for predicting process capability for user-defined tolerances using CBR. Given the upper and lower tolerances (U.S.L and L.S.L), the system calculates the midpoint and applies nearest neighbor techniques to find the predicted process capability (CPK) from the best matching cases. (See Figure 5.3.) The predicted value is calculated by adapting the CPK value from the past case to fit in with the user's new tolerances.

A user accesses the system to obtain Occurrence values for Process FMEA, again using simple CBR techniques. Occurrence is a qualitative integer value between 1 and 10 that indicates how often the problem is likely to occur. It is a function of CPK, and is obtained from a suitable past case, using the SPC's database as the case-base.

5.3.5   Case Representation

The PCR database is a case base for troubleshooting problems within the foundry. As with all the systems, a conventional database structure

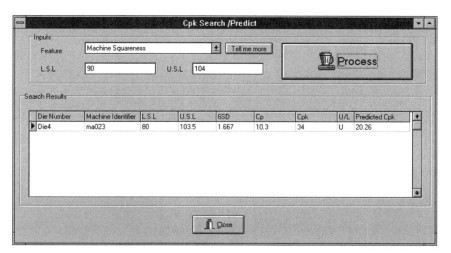

Figure 5.3   The search and predict window from the SPC system.

stores the information. The following EXPRESS description defines all the PCR and 8D information as a single entity.[3] Where not obvious, the data types are plain text.

```
ENTITY QPAC_PCR ABSTRACT SUPERTYPE OF (ONEOF(internal_PCR,customer_PCR));
    PCR_status : PCR_status_type;
    release_date: date;
    due_date: date;
    customer: STRING;
    die_number: STRING;
    part_number: STRING;
    process: Process_type;
    problem: failure_mode_type;
    description: strings;        --textual description of problem
    reaction: reaction_type;     --how the foundry responded to the problem
    occurrence: RPN_type;        --proportion of defective parts (1-10)
    detection: RPN_type;         --how often detected (1-10)
    quantity: whole_number;      --number of parts defective
    (* 8D information *)
    team_members: LIST [1:?] OF foundry_person;
    containment_actions: containment_actions_type;
    root_of_problem: root_problem;
    chosen_actions: chosen_permanent_corrective_actions_type;
    implemented_actions: corrective_actions_type;
    preventive_actions: corrective_actions_type;
    full_8D_required : BOOLEAN;
UNIQUE
    die_number;
WHERE
    problem_ok:
    relevant_failure_mode(process,problem);
END_ENTITY;--end of PCR entity
```

It is important that users feel comfortable entering the information into the system. This is why much of the information stored in the sys-

---

3 EXPRESS is an ISO Standard language for information modeling widely used in manufacturing and design.

tem is textual. Since we did not intend to adapt the retrieved cases this was not a problem.

5.3.6 Case Acquisition

Each foundry had its own stock of past cases stored on paper, based on their own experiences. We decided that combining these into a single database was undesirable since each foundry manufactures different kinds of parts and uses slightly different methods and different machinery. Therefore, each foundry maintains its own case base. The initial set of past cases came from paper-based PCRs and 8D reports. The representation used by the computerized system was closely based on the existing paper-based one; consequently, cases are stored virtually "raw," requiring no further processing.

Since the cases were input by the foundries themselves, much of the knowledge acquisition was automatic. However, we still needed to be able to understand the information ourselves in order to represent it in a sensible way. This requires an understanding of:

- the terminology used,
- the typical kinds of problems involved,
- the interrelationships between the various bits of information, and
- quality procedures.

5.3.7 Case Retrieval

The case-based troubleshooting system uses nearest neighbor retrieval to find the most appropriate cases. The CBR system also employs a parts classification system that assigns numerical values for five quality attributes:

- surface finish (for example, smoothness),
- aesthetic appearance,
- integrity (for example, lack of porosity),
- cleanliness (for example, lack of swarf/flash), and
- stability (for example, strength).

Each of the five quality attributes takes on a qualitative value, which represents the level of importance of the attribute. The part classification options give sensible default values to begin with. The user can then fine-tune the attributes to give values that are more appropriate for the current PCR. The quality attributes are then used in conjunction with nearest neighbor matching to retrieve past-case PCRs. The default quality attributes are derived from a component hierarchy that orders the matched cases so that the most likely cases will be those as close as possible in the hierarchy to the problem.

The case-based system within the PCR system uses nearest neighbor matching to retrieve cases. The properties (and limitations) of nearest neighbor matching are well understood, but the system is flexible enough to allow users to configure the system so that the best possible match can be achieved with only a couple of attempts. Furthermore, since the system retrieves a list of cases instead of just one, users can judge which one is best.

5.3.8 Case Adaptation and Retention

Information is stored in the PCR system in a very raw state, as detailed textual descriptions that contain specific technical details such as measurements. It is considerably less difficult for users, even with limited foundry experience, to perform their own adaptation than to implement some form of automated adaptation. Automation would have required a much more complex case structure that would have been difficult for foundry personnel to use. For this reason adaptation is not used within the troubleshooting system.

Being a database system, and a replacement for a paper-based system, cases are added to the PCR as a by-product of existing quality procedures. The process is entirely automatic, requiring no preprocessing whatsoever.[4]

---

4 In this system every new case is retained; there is no review process.

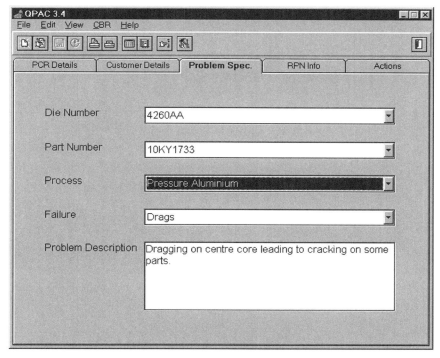

Figure 5.4   Main window of the PCR system.

5.3.9 Interface Design, Testing, and Rollout

A great deal of effort went into designing the user interface for the PCR system. The Delphi software development environment made it possible to create demo interfaces in a very short amount of time that were shown to foundry personnel for review and comment. After a few trials the "tabbed notebook" style of user interface (see Figure 5.4) was adopted, as it let us display a large amount of data with more compactness than the earlier attempts, which used many separate forms. We adopted the same interface style at various levels within the other systems.

As previously mentioned, we delivered the systems to the foundries at various stages throughout the course of the project. In addition to the users in the foundries using the program, we were able to gather realistic data from the foundries and use this to test the systems for ourselves. Because of the way we delivered the software, it was quite natural for a great deal of feedback to come from the foundries, which in turn led to many enhancements to the system.

The case bases are unique to each site. Had the case base been global we would have had problems with some of the terminology, which is also local to each site. Although each of the case bases is now quite large, it is useful for users to be familiar with the dies that relate to them. This is because it will give users greater confidence in the system's ability to retrieve suitable cases.

5.4 System Demonstration

The PCR system is designed to be as user-friendly as possible. For example, when users select a die number from a drop-down list, the program automatically fills in the part number as well as the customer's name and address. Alternatively, users can fill in the part number first, and the other three fields are filled in automatically. This is an important feature for two reasons.

First, it reduces the amount of information that the user has to look up and type in. Second, the information that is immediately at hand will depend on the source of the reported problem. If the customer reported the problem, the user may not know the die number, but if the foundry reported the problem, the user would have to look up the part number. The program prints out PCRs and 8D reports by interacting with Microsoft Word. In addition, the PCR system has features that automate the sending of acknowledgment faxes to the customer, and for producing part analyses, pie charts, and so on, for viewing PCR-related statistics.

When a problem occurs with a part, a new PCR needs to be input into the system. The problem may have been raised by the customer or by the foundry itself. Either way the method is the same. The user selects New PCR from the menu and types in the information required on each page, and then saves the PCR. A separate form lets the user select an existing PCR for viewing or editing (shown in Figure 5.5).

The system helps the user find a case-based match to the PCR currently being viewed; simply selecting Similar Cases from the menu does this. A form showing a progress bar is displayed for a few seconds while case retrieval takes place. The form showing the matched cases is then displayed (see Figure 5.6). If users wish to change the parameters, they can access these from the Advanced tab and then click on the Find Cases button to try again. The Breakdown button displays a form that illustrates numerically how well each parameter of the selected case matched against the original PCR.

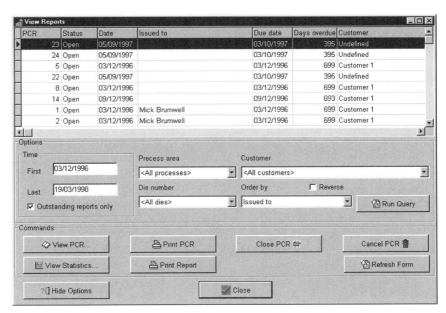

Figure 5.5 The View Reports form of the PCR system.

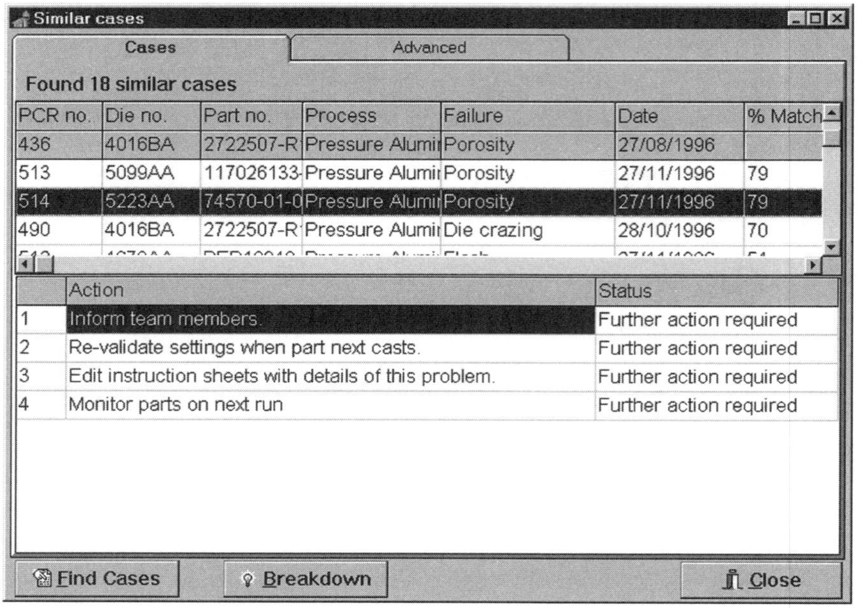

Figure 5.6   The case-matching tool of the PCR system.

5.5 Benefits

Currently each foundry has about 200 PCRs in their database. The addition of cases to the system replaces the old quality procedure that involved writing out a PCR and 8D report by hand and circulating it among foundry personnel. It should be obvious therefore that the new system represents a considerable time saving, since the foundry personnel can access *all* the PCRs from any PC terminal on site.

Using CBR provides the cornerstone for helping us to build up, manage, and reuse troubleshooting knowledge to improve product quality in the foundries. It provides excellent data for creating a realistic Process FMEA report and, even beyond that, for deciding on inspection and control checks in the foundry itself.

The individual benefits of the PCR system are:

- *Improved quality control.* Structured recording of foundry problems and their solutions provides the foundry quality manager with clear, well-classified information about the main issues with production within the foundry.
- *More effective troubleshooting.* Efficient access to records of past performance means that experience is not lost. Past solutions are always available to help with present problems.
- *Realistic FMEA reports.* If FMEA reports are written without reference to live foundry data, they can be divorced from the real problems faced in the foundry. The incorporation of the case-based data means that the design analysis for new products is grounded in real foundry experience.

As a whole, the system closes the loop between today's problems of manufacturing and tomorrow's designs, moving the foundry toward problem-free production.

5.6   Conclusion

Knowledge management methodologies such as CBR can be usefully employed for troubleshooting and retrieval of knowledge for other purposes. The raw material for a case-based knowledge management system can often be found in existing paper-based systems. The QPAC PCR system and Wayland are examples of systems that have been built based on existing foundry knowledge from paper files.[5]

Quality systems can be implemented more effectively if designed as part of an integrated set of tools. Statistical records, troubleshooting data, and process design can be useful sources for other systems such as automation of Process FMEA.

---

5 The Wayland system is described in my previous book: *Applying Case-Based Reasoning: Techniques for Enterprise Systems.* Published by Morgan Kaufmann, 1997.

Benchmarking Best Practice

Internal Financial Control at Deloitte Touche[1]

Olivier Curet
Deloitte Touche Tohmatsu

6.1 Introduction

Deloitte & Touche is one of the U.K.'s largest firms of chartered accountants and management consultants, with twenty-four offices and over 6,500 staff nationwide. The U.K. practice of Deloitte Touche Tohmatsu (DTT) is a global leader in professional services with over 72,000 employees in 129 countries. With the mergers and acquisitions

---

1 The views expressed in this chapter are the author's own, and not necessarily those of Deloitte Touche Tohmatsu (DTT) or any national practice thereof. No legal liability is accepted by the author, DDT, or Deloitte & Touche for any use made of this work. The author wishes to thank Laurence Capus for her contribution to a first draft of this chapter.

of recent years, and the drive to generate new business, the international firm has been able to consolidate its position as a leading practice, with worldwide fee income of over $7 billion. DTT provides a range of services delivered through specialist, multifunctional teams, designed to meet the requirements of the principal business sectors that we serve. These teams, which are organized on a national basis, can draw on a complete range of assurance and advisory, tax, corporate finance, reorganization, insolvency, forensic, management solutions, management consultancy, and other business services, thus bringing together our expertise in each sector to benefit clients.

We are one of the global leaders for audits of the world's largest companies, and our largest clients include major companies from all industry sectors. This chapter explains the use of CBR in a specific business problem domain, namely, internal control evaluation, drawing on the experience from Deloitte & Touche UK.

6.2 The Problem

The Cadbury Committee established the UK Code of Best Practice on Corporate Governance for business in 1992. The Code of Best Practice states that UK company directors should report on the "effectiveness" of their company's system of internal control. An opinion on the effectiveness of the system of internal control is not required, but an increasing number of UK companies give such an opinion.

However, there was no general guidance on how these reports on effectiveness should be done or even on the form or content of the reports until a Joint Working Group produced the "Internal Control and Financial Reporting" document in December 1994. This document focused more on a subset of internal control, namely, internal financial control. The principles explained in this document have been relevant to all UK business enterprises. The "Internal Control and Financial Reporting" document described some general principles, but the exact formats of companies' directors' statements were not prescribed, although it was suggested they might appear in separate statements or other reports than financial reports.

Since then it has been recommended that annual reports for UK companies include specific statements: these statements should confirm that the company's directors are responsible for the company's system of internal financial control. The statements also should describe the key control elements that the directors have set up, warn that these key control elements can only give "reasonable and not absolute assurance against material misstatement or loss," and attest that directors have reviewed the effectiveness of the system of internal financial control.

The different criteria for assessing effectiveness may be categorized as:

- *The company's control environment.* These elements may include controls regarding management involvement in business operations and monitoring progress, control over transactions, adequacy of division of responsibilities, and appropriateness of planning and implementation.

- *Identification and evaluation of risks and control objectives.* These elements may include controls over the appropriateness of business systems and risk analysis processes.

- *Monitoring and corrective action.* These elements may include the level of compliance with control criteria, reviews and checks, levels of reconciliations, scope and frequency of evaluations, and appropriateness of internal audit.

- *Information and communication.* These elements may include appropriateness of flows of internal and external information, use of IT, completeness and timeliness of information, and appropriateness of follow-up actions by management.

- *Control procedures.* These elements may include control over violations of relevant laws and regulations, general computer controls including access to data, control over financials (such as treasury, credit given to customers, inventory, etc.), and cash management in general.

■ *Appropriateness of reporting.* These elements may include appropriateness of reporting approaches, processes of reporting to the Board, reporting of legal and accounting developments to senior management, and exception reporting.

Although these criteria may seem to be quite comprehensive, the "Internal Control and Financial Reporting" guidance did not include examples of how statements by company directors on internal financial control should be made. However, the same guidance advises that the company statements should include an explanation of the steps taken by the company to:

■ ensure an appropriate control environment,
■ state the processes used to identify major business risks,
■ assess the information technology in place,
■ understand the major control procedures, and
■ explain the monitoring system used by the Board to check that the system is effective.

To summarize, directors of U.K.-based companies are responsible for establishing and maintaining appropriate internal control systems. As there is no general or standardized approach for doing so, judgments must be made not only to assess the anticipated benefits and costs of management information and of control procedures, but also in the control estimation approach itself. As a consequence, an appropriate way to help directors examine on a confidential basis their business's level of internal control is to compare, or benchmark, their operations with other companies, whether these companies are competitors or not. In this way, directors can analyze where their internal control strengths and weaknesses are most significant so that action can be taken to establish and maintain appropriate internal control systems.

Rule-based artificial intelligence techniques have helped Deloitte & Touche clients to design and run applications in business areas where decision making has been relatively well structured and easily transferable into formalized rule-based models.[2] The fact that standard business procedures are frequently highly structured or semistructured has spawned the initial rush of successful rule-based applications. However, the situation is different when dealing with unstructured business domains such as internal control, where expertise is scarce, expensive, and difficult to formalize.

There is still a need to support business decision making for internal control, as it is a problem domain not bounded by rules, although there are as many different cases of internal controls as there are companies. Any rule-based processing to tackle internal control evaluation would raise some doubt, as rules do not lend themselves to capturing tacit knowledge of volatile business domains dynamically and combining different experts' views. Most of the present business expertise in internal control evaluation exists in the form of cases rather than procedures that can be more easily converted into rules. One means of approaching the problem of translating procedures would be a solution consisting of the provision of a case library of expertise. CBR is well suited for this approach for the reasons explained in the next section.

6.3 The Knowledge Management Solution

CBR is an appropriate approach to deal with internal control since experience drawn from specific business case studies is in most instances more valuable than generalized textbook knowledge. At the same time, internal control evaluation is a domain where there is a potential combinatorial explosion because of the existence of many features associated with each case of internal control. By finding the case closest to a specific business under evaluation, CBR shows the key questions that lead to benchmarking the problem, rather than a

---

2 This can be done where explicit, easily codified knowledge was available.

battery of standard parameters that may have nothing to do with the problem.

Accountants investigating adequacy of levels of internal controls rely more frequently on examples than rules, especially when the repository of knowledge lies in the informal domain. As there are no generally accepted and reliable rules for internal controls, accountants often have to rely on hints, clues, or assumptions.[3] Until now, expertise in internal control evaluation has been developed by the continual confrontation of the accountant with many varied business cases, and the clues for evaluating internal controls lie hidden in large information bases. As there are often similarities in different business cases, if presented to the accountant, these similarities can help not only support but also corroborate judgment. In those instances, cases are often used to validate and even justify the experts' views. In this way, a CBR approach can support a consistent level of business decisions.

A CBR approach in internal control can also be most helpful since this problem domain evolves very rapidly as business patterns change continuously. CBR makes the process of acquiring internal control examples more natural, and obtaining high-level rules of thumb or heuristic knowledge about the domain is made easier. Case-based input avoids the translation of auditing rules of thumb into inference mechanisms that may lead to inconsistencies or loss of tacit knowledge. Case-based input also allows accountants to relate to typical or atypical cases rather than to hypothetical models.[4]

The CBR model allows business cases of internal controls to be deleted as they become obsolete, and fictitious cases may be added to complete the coverage of the problem domain. Using past illustrations of internal controls, business experts will, in most examples, prefer to

---

3 These are examples of tacit knowledge.
4 This is a good example of cases being used as contextualized stories, rich in circumstantial detail that would be lost if the knowledge they contained were translated into a formalized representation.

refer to these cases by using idea association. Indeed, the confidence in the CBR application will tend to increase in such circumstances.

6.3.1 Expected Benefits

One of the main reasons for using CBR at Deloitte & Touche for business domains such as internal controls, and fraud detection in particular, is that the case-based model explicitly combines searching with learning.[5] Using CBR in internal control evaluation can give users access to deeper knowledge and more relevant reasoning about the problem in the form of a data laboratory exercise.

For example, in browsing a cluster tree discriminating between internal control cases, the user observes the discriminators or nodes that are most information-rich, or meaning-rich. These meaning-rich aspects of a case-based approach may be crucial to the user for a more appropriate level of interaction, by which the user is encouraged to explore the problem domain until an appropriate solution is generated from the search and learn processes. By recollecting past cases of internal control, reasoning can be directed because there is a comprehensive path or trail laid out along which ideas and concepts naturally flow. In contrast to the result orientation of traditional rule-based approaches (where in most instances only a tracing facility is available), the case-based searching and learning approach has a critic-orientation emphasis.

Both rule-based and CBR systems may contribute to increased consistency in business decision making in different ways: traditional systems have attempted to automate activities where business expertise is crucial, whereas CBR can be applied in business areas for which human intelligence needs to be augmented and amplified.

---

5 A fraud detection system implemented using CBR by Deloitte & Touche is described in my previous book: *Applying Case-Based Reasoning: Techniques for Enterprise Systems*, Morgan Kaufmann, 1997.

Expertise enhancement has been one of the major drivers behind the ControlSCAPE application designed by Deloitte & Touche.

Learning about internal control is a crucial ingredient in the reasoning process, but often learning requires several iterations of problem solving and restructuring of business knowledge in the light of new experiences. Human problem solving in loosely structured business domains may falter when people must rely on memory to retrieve appropriate solved cases. This is especially true for experts whose heuristic reasoning depends on patterns of data embedded in past business cases.

For these reasons, it also makes sense that ControlSCAPE could accelerate knowledge transfer, help staff share experiences, and also preserve knowledge gained in the corporate environment. These aspects are especially relevant to people dealing with unstructured business knowledge, since a large part of their tasks relies not only on objective information but also subjective interpretation of it. It is in this context that Deloitte & Touche decided to design ControlSCAPE either as a *directing* system (using internal control cases to provide the user with simple adapted solutions from past cases relevant to the case under scrutiny) or as an *indicating* system (giving the user an opportunity to discover knowledge from cases that are "neighboring" the problem).

In this way, ControlSCAPE would emphasize accountants' analogical problem solving and as a consequence help them reach more informed decisions about appropriateness of systems of internal control. ControlSCAPE was designed to encourage accountants' *imitation* (applying solutions to the current problem by referring to past solved cases), *opinion making* (searching for a clue that could lead to a solution to the problem), and *insight* (giving a greater understanding of the problem domain by scanning through pertinent cases). Thus, the case-based analogical reasoning in internal control provides an opportunity for the business user to justify and support his or her decision when the domain is too complex or when there is a need for conflict resolution, which could eventually cost the client dearly.

6.3.2   The Team

The team consisted of the partner in charge (Martyn Jones, National Audit Technical Partner for the U.K. firm) and a member of staff (Olivier Curet, Senior Manager), supported by several consultants. The product champions have had extensive experience with the use of CBR and have been a driving force in the U.K. firm behind the design, implementation, and evaluation of specific knowledge-based systems and especially case-based approaches to business problem domains. These problem domains have included the detection of management fraud, the detection of transfer pricing strategies, the identification of invoice discounting strategies, and the evaluation of trade missions.

6.3.3   Implementation Plan

The first part of the methodology consisted of case feature definition. Deloitte & Touche had already designed a method called "ICAP" (Initial Case Acquisition Process) used during our previous CBR-related work for applications mentioned earlier. The role of ICAP was to construct a set of potential case descriptors by circulating a questionnaire that collected key features from the firm's top experts. Initially, the features suggested arose from past cases, which allowed accountants to input their knowledge in a less constrained way. The resulting set of features was then recirculated to permit the experts to change, amend, or delete any features they felt were inappropriate, and the process was repeated until the different experts agreed. The amended form was circulated again to all the experts who crafted the questions in the first place, until the final version was agreed (validated). This "semi-Delphic" process allowed the users and designers to agree on the features that should be used to characterize cases and also to decide the types of cases that should be collected.

After the feature calibration was validated, ICAP made it necessary to collect further cases on the basis of the agreed set. The purpose of this "case stabilization" was to collect a sufficient number of cases to obtain an appropriate coverage of the problem domain. Issues such as the effects of case aggregation (for example, is there a target number of cases to collect?) and case duplication (for example, what should be done about redundant cases?) were tackled. Thereafter, the reference case evolved with use over time, and the application was tested continuously as it expanded.

Once the ControlSCAPE case base was stabilized, it became the case library, and the application was ready for implementation. (The system architecture is shown in Figure 6.1.) The most appropriate method of case retrieval was decided. This included deciding the relative importance (or weights) of features in case retrievals and whether weight vectors should be prescribed or left open for users to choose. The flexibility of querying the case library was also examined. Other is-

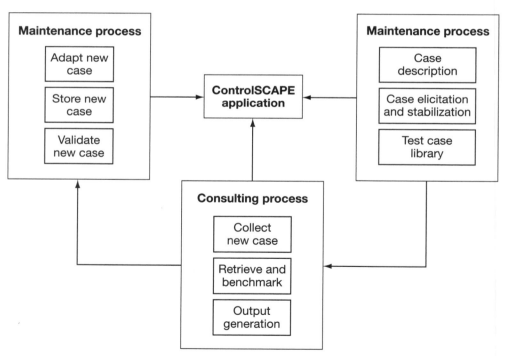

Figure 6.1 System processes.

sues examined included case adaptation, when a new case should be stored and by whom, who is responsible for ensuring that the system has been "trained," what kind of user training is required, and who should be responsible for the continuous evaluation of the system. The ControlSCAPE Development Group's role was to coordinate the overall process and collect cases.

6.3.4   Hardware and Software

We evaluated several CBR development tools and examined how our major competitors used CBR within knowledge management processes. Five of the six main accounting and consulting firms are known to use CBR. These are Deloitte Touche Tohmatsu (audit), Andersen Consulting (linking CBR and virtual reality), KPMG and PriceWaterhouseCoopers (help desks), and Coopers & Lybrand (risk and control). Deloitte & Touche (U.K.) and Coopers & Lybrand (Germany) used the ReMind CBR tool, while the other firms used eGain's CBR tools.[6]

As part of the ControlSCAPE project, it was necessary to choose either to have a complete in-house system or to build an application with an existing CBR tool. The advantages of using an off-the-shelf tool allowed the ControlSCAPE Development Group to focus on the methodology, case collection, and subsequent customization to client requirements. Programming a full CBR application, including the creation of retrieval algorithms and user interface, would have significantly increased the risks associated with the project (such as going over budget or over time).

The functionality required by ControlSCAPE was the capacity to retrieve cases using advanced retrieval strategies (based on induction rather than nearest neighbor), and the capacity to allow the fine-tuning of case representation (by defining symbolic values, for example).

---

6 A list of CBR tool vendors is given in the Appendix.

ReMind had already been successfully used in the firm during the early 1990s for prototypes. It was felt that for working on a standalone basis, for a very specific business problem, and working with a centralized case library, ReMind had the functionalities we were looking for despite its drawbacks. The system can run on a standard notebook computer.

6.3.5 Case Acquisition

During the ControlSCAPE case-base design phase, internal control cases were carefully defined and collected to ensure coverage of the business problem domain. To start with, the first part of the ICAP process was the result of a brainstorming session with several of the firm's top experts in the audit field, mainly from U.K. and U.S. firms. Specific discriminators about internal controls emerged from this exercise; and after several sessions over a few weeks, some specific questions were repeated and patterns emerged when experts were asked to think about past cases. At the end of this first process, the series of questions that had been formulated were clustered around the Cadbury Report framework, including:

- control environment,
- identification and evaluation of risk,
- monitoring and corrective action,
- information and communication,
- control procedures, and
- other.

Structured interviews took place during the following part of the ICAP process. The selected audit experts were asked to fill in the questionnaire while thinking about past cases they had encountered, and to walk through it with the interviewer. Initially they were asked to talk about the general principles driving good or bad levels of internal controls, discern between several types of internal control environments, and relate these types to general audit principles.

After this process, the following five questions were asked:

1. Are the indicators of "good" or "bad" internal controls exhaustive? If not, please give an exhaustive list.
2. How do you find out about these "good" or "bad" internal controls? Directly, or through an intermediary or manager?
3. In general, what makes you happy that nothing unusual is going on?
4. In general, what would alert you to types of unusualness?
5. Is there anything that is so universal an indicator of "good" or "bad" internal controls that it and it alone will cause you to rethink your approach to an audit? Please list the indicators.

It was also possible for interviewees to express their thoughts while completing the exercise. The process was set to last no longer than forty-five minutes and was conducted by individuals with little background knowledge of internal controls: this way, an interviewer who had some knowledge of the domain could not lead the interviewee, or disagree with the interviewee's comments during the interviews. In this specific way, ICAP was used to define the criteria being used for each question and as a consequence to define more closely the case representation.

6.3.6 Case Representation

ControlSCAPE works on the basis of the interviewees' perceptions of internal control matters, ranked from 0 (low) to 5 (high) using a modified Likert scale. One example question with its scale is shown in Figure 6.2.

Figure 6.2 A Likert scale question.

By representing and designing ControlSCAPE questions, it was discovered very early during the ICAP process that it was necessary to make a distinction on the questionnaire between the "true" and the "false" missing values. The true missing value (for example, N/A) is a value that is not available because it is not applicable to the case being collected. For example, a question refers to internal audit and there is no internal audit function. The false missing value (for example, IK—insufficient knowledge) is used for a question that is applicable to the case, but the accountant does not know the answer or cannot remember. For example, his or her investigations were not yet advanced enough to answer this question.

The difference between the two is essential for two main reasons. First, it allows the discrimination between data that is not available but is still useful during the use of ControlSCAPE. Second, when the feedback to clients is given, one of the first areas of concern may be to perform further investigation for which the answers are IK. As a consequence, two extra missing value categories were added to the questionnaire during the ICAP process, representing, respectively, not applicable and insufficient knowledge.

It has been shown that experts are quite poor at weighting information accurately and that their answers to specific questions affect their measurement of other questions. Whenever experts give judgmental answers to soft issues, there is no way to split statistically the valid from the biased elements. This is why an overall evaluation field has been added to ControlSCAPE. This "heuristic link" could be statistically measured, but it would be difficult to validate. For these reasons ControlSCAPE does not try to explain possible correlations between subjective answers. The overall perception field is illustrated in Figures 6.3 and 6.4.

6.3.7 Case Retrieval

ControlSCAPE includes a full list of features on internal controls (more than 350 parameters for 200 cases as of May 1998). Figure 6.5 provides a representative list of case features.

In your opinion which of the following case types best descibes the client?	
Seriously inadequate internal control	1
Underdeveloped internal control	2
Potential problems with internal control	3
Company is regarded as having adequate internal control	4
Well-developed internal control	5
Internal control is perceived as very well developed and progressive	6
"World class" internal control	7

Figure 6.3   Case types.

How would you rate each of the following elements of the entity's control structure?	
	Grading
Control enviroment	1 2 3 4 5 6 7
Identification and evaluation of risk	1 2 3 4 5 6 7
Monitoring and corrective action including internal audit	1 2 3 4 5 6 7
Information and communication	1 2 3 4 5 6 7
Control activities	1 2 3 4 5 6 7

Figure 6.4   Control element types.

ControlSCAPE uses both induction and nearest neighbor retrieval, but only results from nearest neighbor searches are given back to clients (in the form of averaged similarities of the ten nearest neighbors).

6.3.8   Case Adaptation

ControlSCAPE does no case adaptation. The problem is that appropriate CBR adaptation approaches depend on the purpose of the

Control environment	
q100 Extent to which board approves significant proposals	1 2 3 4 5 N/A I/K
q101 Coherence of board	1 2 3 4 5 N/A I/K
...	1 2 3 4 5 N/A I/K
Identification and evaluation of risk	
q300 Extent to which new and changing risks are clearly identified and reported to board	1 2 3 4 5 N/A I/K
q301 Extent to which areas of responsibility are well defined	1 2 3 4 5 N/A I/K
...	1 2 3 4 5 N/A I/K
Monitoring and corrective action including internal audit	
q400 Extent to which board monitors high-risk areas	1 2 3 4 5 N/A I/K
q401 Extent to which control framework includes monitoring	1 2 3 4 5 N/A I/K
...	1 2 3 4 5 N/A I/K
Information and communication	
q500 Extent to which mechanisms are in place to obtain relevant external information—on market conditions, competitors' programs, legislative or regulatory developments, and economic changes	1 2 3 4 5 N/A I/K
q501 Extent to which internally generated information critical to achievement of the entity's objectives, including that of critical success factors, is identified and regularly reported	1 2 3 4 5 N/A I/K
...	1 2 3 4 5 N/A I/K
Control activities	
q600 Extent to which the owner/manager/president is interested in controls	1 2 3 4 5 N/A I/K
q601 Extent to which the owner gets involved in the detail	1 2 3 4 5 N/A I/K
...	1 2 3 4 5 N/A I/K
Other	
q700 Extent to which influence of family/relatives on board is avoided	1 2 3 4 5 N/A I/K
q701 Extent to which business is keeping pace with technology	1 2 3 4 5 N/A I/K
...	1 2 3 4 5 N/A I/K

Figure 6.5   Representative list of ControlSCAPE features.

system and its desired outcome. Cases of internal control can be seen as being too instrumental and only flat descriptions or snapshots of past instances, the definitions or even contexts of which may no longer be relevant to any business. If all the data is quantitative, CBR and its adaptation process may be relatively straightforward. In contrast, it is far less easy to adapt business cases when the domain knowledge contains soft information, such as an expert's judgments and perceptions, rather than hard, or factual, data.

The generation of soft information-based business cases is used more to guide and suggest user reasoning and learning based on some relevant cases. If the cases contain mainly soft information, adaptation may be mainly user guided. In contrast, if the cases contain mainly factual descriptions of past cases, they can be directly adapted to solve the present problem.

6.3.9   Case Retention and Maintenance

Maintenance issues include deciding when a case becomes obsolete, when new cases and/or features need to be added, and the criteria that dictate when to store a new case. Only the case base administrator is authorized to maintain the case base. This greatly reduces the risks associated with possible interference from other users who may input cases or delete previous ones unknowingly. Training has been given to other managers who can also operate the system when the administrator is out of the office. All new cases that are investigated using ControlSCAPE for client assignment are input in the case base on a confidential basis. Only the senior manager or partner in charge of the application is authorized to request that new criteria be added to the application.

6.3.10   Interface Design

There was no specific interface design since the default interface of the ReMind tool was used. This is one advantage of using software that the firm already knew instead of programming and customizing a full application in-house. As the manager in charge of running the system knows the tool very well, it was felt that the interface did not need change, and efforts instead concentrated on case collection, processing, and output generation issues.

6.3.11 Testing

With regard to the evaluation phase, particular attention was given to both the accuracy of the case base (whether relevant cases are retrieved) and usage (whether the correct decisions are reached on the basis of the cases recovered). The approach used for evaluating ControlSCAPE was the same as for previous applications that the firm had built, including the fraud detection system.

The problem with evaluating CBR knowledge management applications is related to the understanding that the validation of the application is more complex than for conventional systems. A CBR application is more difficult to evaluate because new cases are input on a continuous basis and users' expectations change with time. Furthermore, the evaluation of such systems in a business organization is critical because members of management need to know whether the time devoted to the project and the financial investment have been worth it.

A few methods have been designed for CBR evaluation, either after implementation or during the development process. In our domain some business cases may be irrelevant to a particular end user, while different users may perceive the subjectivity inevitably included in cases in different ways. In effect, our CBR knowledge management systems contain layers of different experiences. In some domains, features can encapsulate qualitative details, such as perceptions, understanding, and biases about specific problems. Although cases are not necessarily consistent with one another, they will make up a coherent encapsulation of the problem domain. One major aspect of CBR is that the case base is expanding all the time, so the results of searching the case base are time sensitive and user sensitive. All these factors influence the nature of the *knowledge discovery* process, and thus must be taken into account during evaluation.

Since CBR solves problems by selecting similar problems or similar sequences of events, the business solutions generated may vary more because the cases used represent very different concrete business experiences. This is why a more holistic approach to the evaluation of ControlSCAPE was used, assessing both the accuracy of the system (that is, its reliability) and its effectiveness (its impact on the user and the organization).

The accuracy approach to ControlSCAPE evaluation consisted of testing the number of successful hits (retrieving cases of the same type, on the scale from 1—seriously inadequate levels of control—to 7—world class). It was important to estimate the precision and noise when searching for and retrieving "appropriate" knowledge. The *precision* of information retrieval has been considered as being the ratio of the number of items relevant to the user (hits), divided by the total number of items retrieved. The *noise* of information can be considered as being the ratio of the number of items not relevant to the user (waste), divided by the total number of items retrieved.

6.3.12   Rollout and Benefits

Since ControlSCAPE was tested and validated, it was used in the London office. Initially it was applied to small-sized projects (mainly from the UK). After these few projects, no major amendments were requested. Accountants discovered very early that ControlSCAPE had the following benefits:

- The system enables any business control system to be measured on a scale from 1 to 7, taking the scales from the nearest neighbors. This benchmark is quite difficult to perform without ControlSCAPE.
- ControlSCAPE facilitates internal and external benchmarking. It makes sense to benchmark among business units within the larger

companies, and it also makes sense to benchmark any internal system with peer companies.

- ControlSCAPE enhances judgments relating to quality of systems while identifying where further internal control inquiries need to be made, as well as identifying weaknesses.
- ControlSCAPE can show where improvements in internal controls can be made by measuring the gap between the client's level of control and the "best in class."
- ControlSCAPE output facilitates the governance process by providing succinct overview of strengths and weaknesses to the client company's Board.

6.4 System Demonstration

The ControlSCAPE questionnaire is always completed to the fullest extent possible. The respondents' first impressions are considered the most valuable. It is requested that in the first phases of operation, parameters are neither deleted nor changed. It is advised that the ControlSCAPE questionnaire should take about forty-five minutes to complete if the respondents know the entity or group well. If several people come together to develop and answer shared views, more time will be required to facilitate discussion and consensus.

Every effort is always made to complete the questionnaire in one session. The ControlSCAPE questionnaire may be completed by the accountant as part of a client service engagement or new business initiative, or may be made available to clients to complete their own assessment. In situations where clients complete the questionnaire, responses are reviewed to ensure completeness and responsiveness to the intended control parameters. In all cases, the client service partner reviews the questionnaire for reasonableness and completeness, especially if there are different cases collected about the client's different subsidiaries worldwide.

In completing the questionnaire, it is important to provide background information about the case (type of entity, size of turnover, etc.). This information will enable comparisons to be made not only against the database as a whole but also against specific subsets and combinations within the database, including industry sector, size, nature of the entity, type of entity, or even geographic location. The identities of the entities in the case base are always kept confidential.

After the team of accountants and/or client's senior management have answered the ControlSCAPE questionnaire, the responses are input for benchmarking. The ControlSCAPE output includes a nearest neighbor analysis and profile that indicate which questions and answers were weighed most heavily in determining the cases that the current case most closely resembles. This provides the client with an overall assessment of the internal control structure (whether it is underdeveloped, adequate, well developed, progressive, etc.), suggestions for improvement, and a comparison against industry averages. The typical ControlSCAPE deliverable document includes a benchmarking report (analysis of ten nearest neighbors); graphical display indicating where the company falls on the scale, from seriously inadequate to world class; profiling of key parameters used for analysis; identification of areas of insufficient knowledge; and comparison against average under each of the five Cadbury headings. Figure 6.6 shows a selection of anonymous slides from a recent project.

6.5   Conclusion

ControlSCAPE has shown that CBR is an appropriate approach to business problem solving when the problem domain is unstructured and involves significant amounts of tacit knowledge. The main benefit of ControlSCAPE is the significant added value it gives to Deloitte & Touche clients. The ControlSCAPE techniques, resulting audit work, and discussions always help the client identify control performance gaps. Workshops with clients can then be organized by holding one or

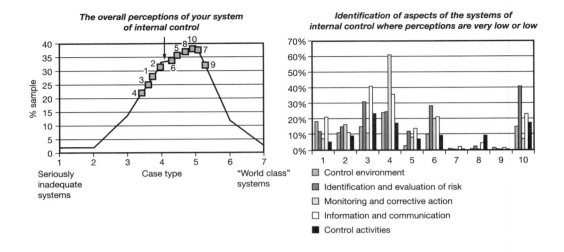

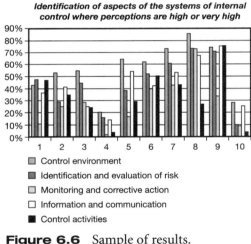

Key areas where improvements may need to be considered

- Emphasis of requesting reports on strategic opportunities and long term objectives
- Improve risk assessment techniques
- Level of staff compliance with Code of Conduct
- Outside parties' awareness of ethical standards
- Physical access controls
- Level of continuity/reliability of outsourced resources
- Extent of controls of business risks and rotation of control roles

Figure 6.6   Sample of results.

more sessions with the client's staff to generate ideas on control performance opportunities. Part of these sessions can be used to identify the change drivers and business objectives and then help brainstorm with the client on the aspects of the system of control that are strong, and on where it can be improved. Potentials for improvement are always detected. A second benchmark can be done as a follow-up a few months after the first benchmark to see if the ratings improve.

7

Information Retrieval
Intelligent Online Product Selection for Analog Devices

Sean Breen
Interactive Multimedia Systems
Michel Manago
Kaidara International
Stefan Wess and Wolfgang Wilke
Empolis Knowledge Management

7.1 Introduction

Analog Devices designs, manufactures, and markets a broad line of high-performance linear, mixed-signal, and digital integrated circuits (ICs) that address a wide range of real-world signal processing applications. The company's principal products include system-level ICs and general-purpose, standard product linear ICs. Other products include devices manufactured using assembled product technology, such as hybrids, which combine unpackaged IC chips and other chip-level components in a single package.

With sales of $1.2 billion for the last fiscal year, Analog Devices is a leading provider of precision high-performance integrated circuits used in analog and digital signal processing applications. Headquartered in Norwood, Massachusetts, the company employs more than 7,000 people worldwide and has manufacturing facilities in the United States, Ireland, the Philippines, and Taiwan.

Interactive Multimedia Systems (IMS), with their partners Empolis and Kaidara International, built a solution for an electronic catalogue on a CD-ROM together with a Web solution for the product selection of operational amplifiers for Analog Devices in the United States. In this chapter we will describe this solution as one example of a successful knowledge management application in the area of e-commerce.

7.2   The Problem

Analog Device's largest single product group is general-purpose standard linear ICs, which include data converters and amplifiers. Analog Devices has also become a major digital signal processing IC supplier, providing both general-purpose DSPs and highly integrated application-specific devices that combine analog and digital signal-processing capability in a single IC.

The availability of technical information, knowledge, and competent consultancy are crucial for the successful sales of the company's electronic circuits. Therefore, Analog Devices provides online information on the applicability of its products. Conventional databases can only search for exact criteria. Thus, in many cases customer support experts are still required. The solution that has been provided enables users to specify the circuit required for their application. Using knowledge of tolerances, the system identifies those Analog products that best meet users' requirements. The intelligent search capabilities and their availability on the Web are unique selling points for Analog. Additional benefits include increased customer satisfaction and reduced information provision costs.

Within a product line, most of Analog Device's products are different from each other only by one element, and they are described by up to forty parameters. (See Figure 7.1.) Technical support engineers take customers' requirements over the phone and try to find a match in the Analog Devices product range—a complex process that involves weighting dozens of constraints while interacting with the customers and trying to understand their real priorities. This is a lengthy process that can only be successfully accomplished by knowledgeable and well-trained engineers.

Analog Devices tried using SQL-style searches, but these only return a result when all conditions are exactly met. When customers provide a complete set of specifications, the most likely answer is "no match found," and when they relax some of the specifications, hundreds of matches are found.

Customers must have confidence that their transactions will be secure and confidential, and they want assurances that they will not be subject to liability. Shopping on the Web must be convenient—as simple to use and as ubiquitous as ATMs. Finally, there must be incentives to purchase goods via the Internet, whether because of better prices, service, or selection.

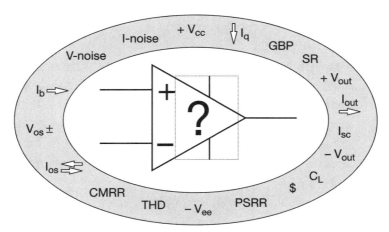

Figure 7.1   How to select the most appropriate amplifier.

E-commerce development has focused almost exclusively on the transactional elements of the sales process. As a result, there is now a range of convenient and secure technologies on the Web for buying and selling products. But how do buyers select the product they want, particularly when many hundreds of similar products are offered, as in Analog's case?

Today, searching for information or the right products on the Web is a complex task, both for consumers and businesses. Unlike a real-world store, no intelligent support or assistance is available on the Web to help customers select products or navigate through product information and alternatives. The product-oriented databases and index-oriented product catalogues that are widely used look and feel just like their paper-based counterparts. Thus, they offer no added value to customers.

Because of the Web's interactive nature, e-commerce solutions can overcome these deficits. Customers can customize the system to suit their special requirements and preferences while searching for the products that best suit their needs. Imagine that you want to find a place to live. You will probably have a number of essential basic requirements, then desirable priorities, and finally, optional desirable features. Consider this example: "I am looking for a four-bedroom detached house. Two bathrooms are essential. I would like at least a quarter acre, close to or in a town. It must be within two hours of Paris. Gas central heating is preferable. I would like a house that is less than twenty years old. I do not like bungalows." A search through a typical Realtor's database would certainly fail to find a house that best meets your requirements; it simply could not handle a complex query like this. Under normal circumstances this type of request could only be dealt with in person by an agent who could weigh your requirements against the houses on his or her list. Case-based reasoning offers a solution to handle this type of complex query, and it does it over the Web.[1]

---

1 An online example of CBR being used in a Realtor's office can be seen at www.hookemacdonald.ie.

CBR enables the user to choose which parameters are important, it supports matching based upon similarity (it knows that some values are more similar than others), it weighs each requirement, and it comes up with the products that are most similar to the customer's demands.

Progressive enterprises support their clients and customers during sales with electronic media. Product selection, ordering, and payment are more efficient and cheaper within such solutions. Electronic product catalogues are replacing their paper-based counterparts. However, the huge potential of the new media is often not used to its full extent. To map the paper-based catalogues on a CD-ROM or to place a product database on the Internet does not use the full advantages of the new electronic medium, namely, intelligence and interaction.

CBR applies knowledge management techniques to provide intelligent services and selection tools for e-commerce. It lets designers of electronic stores use both sales knowledge and corporate knowledge to guide customers during the entire sales process. The advantages are:

- Corporate knowledge is applied to advise customers during sales, and as a result even incomplete and vague queries lead to appropriate products.
- Convenient product search ensures customer satisfaction because electronic shops deliver an enhanced service with intelligent content.
- E-commerce applications improve significantly, and customers see shopping online as a real advantage.

Prospective customers who want to purchase products often do not use the same terminology as the product catalogues or product databases use. Furthermore, they do not have complete knowledge about the products and their usage. Corporate knowledge is needed to navigate through the diverse product lines to find the most suitable one. Virtual sales assistance by CBR supports customers with intelligent advice during product selection and delivers intelligent support during sales in e-commerce.

7.3 The Knowledge Management Solution

The solution of a Web server and a CD-ROM with a product catalogue was provided by the consortium using Kaidara's and Empolis's CBR products.[2] The CBR solution is available for Analog Devices' operational amplifiers and data converters. The system is available to customers both as a CD-ROM catalogue and via the Web as part of the Analog Devices Web site.

Using nearest neighbor retrieval technology, a working prototype was developed in less than six months. The new system allows customers to interactively specify their product requirements, and it finds the product that comes closest to meeting all their needs. Values can be numbers or information such as "the best," "sort of," or "less than." The CBR system will always provide an answer: a list of the top ten Analog Devices products that are closest to meeting the specified requirements is produced. If the user is not satisfied, another search will be started with new priorities until the right product is found.

7.3.1 Expected Benefits

With almost a thousand products, Analog Devices was annually printing catalogues and data sheets up to two feet thick. The cost of printing and shipping catalogues to its 50,000 customers worldwide was between $2 million and $3 million per year. The support engineers process an average of forty requests a day. Fifty percent of them deal with the selection of appropriate products for customer applications. The other half deal with technical support for the use of the products.

Analog Devices expects to save $2 million a year, since the cost of producing and shipping CD-ROMs is far less expensive than that of the old paper version. Moreover, the quality of the service provided by the CBR system makes a real difference in this competitive market. Now when customers call sales support, they usually know exactly

---

2 Contact details of CBR software vendors can be found in the Appendix.

what they want, and what they are ordering is exactly what they need. For the support engineer this means having more time to concentrate on really complex customer problems.

Since the system can keep track of the customer's requests, a future extension of the system will be to analyze this valuable marketing information and input it to the design of new products.

7.3.2 The Team

The solution was provided by consultants from Interactive Multimedia Systems, Empolis, and Kaidara International.

7.3.3 System Architecture

Figure 7.2 shows the functional units and data paths of Analog Devices' operational amplifier intranet server. The CBR search server

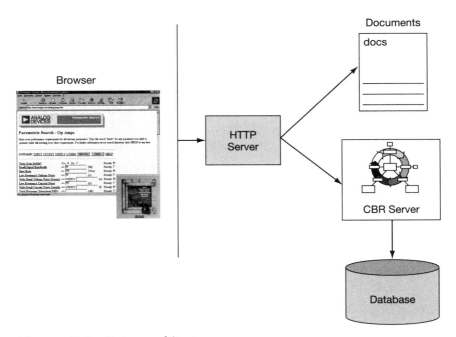

Figure 7.2 System architecture.

generates the HTML representations of the query form and the search results. It provides links to explanations of the individual parameters of the operational amplifiers and to data sheets containing more detailed information about the products. A part of the HTML user interface is shown later, in Section 7.4.

The user's query is preprocessed by the PSS and forwarded to the CBR server. The preprocessing stage, for example, normalizes numerical values with units, such as 5mV, to scalar values like 0.005. The case base, similarity measure, retrieval mechanisms, and other domain-dependent knowledge are handled by the CBR server. The communication between the PSS and the CBR server is established via UNIX Sockets.

7.3.4 Case Representation

The data sheet for an operational amplifier consists of about forty parameters that can be logically structured into objects of parameters modeled in attributes of these objects, such as electrical input and output specifications, functionality, and dimensions. The case model was acquired in several consulting sessions with the technical experts from Analog Devices. Most of the parameter values are high exponent real numbers, but there are also symbolic and textual parameters. The retrieval interface provides hyperlinks to explanations of each of the forty attributes.

The user can influence the priority of every parameter value. The server always returns the ten best matches to the user's query. In this application, only direct product information was modeled. This technical model of sales cases is sufficient because the system is only used by technically skilled customers, who are already experienced clients of Analog Devices. Analog Devices' customers are professional electronic engineers, and they are able to state their demands directly using precise product information.

7.3.5 Case Acquisition

The cases were easy to acquire. All information was available in the technical documents that fully describe each product. The cases were extracted by hand from these documents. Further information was available from the product engineers who designed the products.

7.3.6 Case Retrieval

To assess the similarity of two operational amplifiers, the similarities of all corresponding parameter values are calculated by applying local similarity functions to each pair of corresponding parameters. These local parameter similarities are then used to calculate an overall similarity value for the two devices. From the forty attributes describing the products, thirty-nine have complex similarity measures that represent a part of the product knowledge to support the customers.

The overall similarity is computed as the weighted average of the individual similarities. Subject matter experts in operational amplifiers have suggested the original weight factors, but customers can adjust them according to their priorities. The local similarities for discrete and continuous values are calculated in different ways. Discrete similarity measures are defined in a table that explicitly lists the similarity values for all possible attribute combinations. (See Table 7.1.) This is the (simplified) similarity function for the attribute *maximum temperature range* of an operational amplifier. The symbols *commercial (Com.), industry, military,* and *space* describe temperature range standards of electronic devices.

If, for example, the query specifies *industrial standards,* the CBR system regards *military* and *space* to fulfill the requirements, but

Table 7.1 Example similarity function for discrete attribute values.

Query	Case			
	Com.	Industry	Military	Space
com.	1	1	1	1
industry	0.6	1	1	1
military	0.4	0.6	1	1
space	0.1	0.4	0.6	1

commercial has a similarity of only 0.6. Note that the table is asymmetric: it makes a difference whether the query's attribute value is x and the case's value is y or vice versa. If, for example, the user asks for a device with *industrial standard* temperature specifications, he will be satisfied by a part that fulfills *military* requirements (provided that no other attributes, such as the price, stand against it).

On the other hand, the request for *military standards* cannot be completely satisfied by a part that only has industrial specifications. This situation is reflected by the asymmetry of the similarity table. In general, the table reflects the fact that different temperature standards are subsumed by others, because one standard has a wider range of applicability than another. This knowledge is coded into the similarity measure. This principle also holds for most of the continuous attributes of an operational amplifier.

The only difference is that similarity measures for continuous attributes cannot be as easily represented in a table, but must be formulated as a function. An example of one such similarity function is shown in Figure 7.3, which shows the similarity function for the parameter *current noise density* of an operational amplifier.

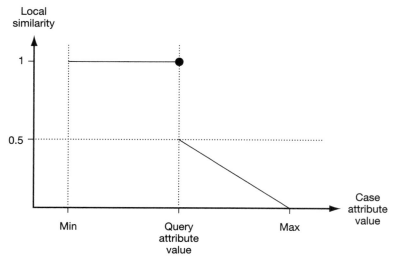

Figure 7.3 A similarity function for continuous attribute values.

The corresponding attribute of a case from the case base has similarity 1.0 if its value is less than or equal to the query's value. Otherwise, the similarity is significantly smaller. The function assumes that there is a minimum and a maximum attribute value. If the case's attribute value is less than or equal to the query attribute's value, their similarity is 1.0. Otherwise it is a value somewhere between 0.0 and 0.5. For certain other attributes the function must be reversed to return 1.0 for values greater than or equal to the query's value and 0.0 to 0.5 for smaller values.

7.3.7   Case Adaptation

This application does not adapt the suggested products because operational amplifiers are unchangeable parts that cannot be reconfigured to the customer's individual demands. The products are fixed, and as a result no modification or adaptation of the suggested products takes place.

7.4   System Demonstration

A typical sales support session works as follows: The customer enters the parameter values he needs into the query form. (See Figure 7.4.) The system will then retrieve the ten best matches to the request. If the results do not exactly fit the customer's needs, the customer can increase the priorities of the parameters that are most important for him. Again, the system displays the ten best matches to the refined query. If the results still do not satisfy the customer, he might fill more parameter slots that he left empty so far, thus further improving the quality of the returned results. Finally, when a suitable device has been found, the customer can link directly to its detailed data sheet. (See Figure 7.5.)

This is very similar to a shop situation when a customer consults the shop assistant: the assistant learns step by step about the customer's exact demands until finally he finds the product that best fits the

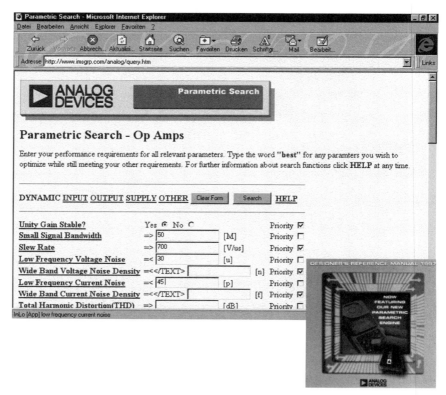

Figure 7.4   Analog devices' query interface.

customer's needs. The CBR system has some of the knowledge of a shop assistant built into it. This knowledge is used to interpret the user's query and greatly enhances the quality of the retrieved data.

However, customers must refine their demands during the iteration of the sales cycle on their own, and they are supported only during retrieval. Nevertheless, even the first request, typically formulated very vaguely, immediately produces usable results. Over- and underspecification, as is typical for common database queries, are avoided. If the system returns more than one answer, the results are ranked by their similarity to the query. This makes it easy for users to refine their request until they are satisfied with the results. In addition to the cus-

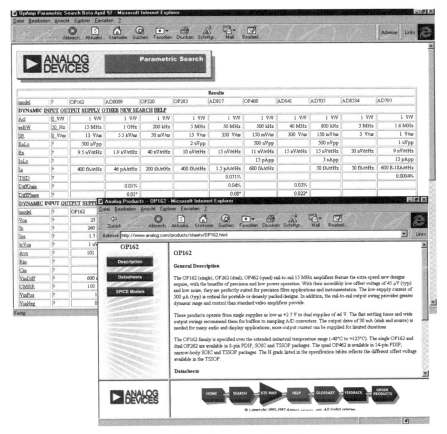

Figure 7.5   Analog devices' product search result.

tomer gains from this intelligent sales-supporting catalogue, this approach will be pursued further to allow some of Analog Devices' engineers to spend more time addressing complex customer support requirements.

Encouraged by the first success of the new CBR catalogue, Analog Devices has decided to extend the application of CBR technology to other product families. Work on these follow-up projects is already under way. One example is the finalized CD-ROM that uses this medium with the same similarity-based search engines for product selection for customers.

7.5   Benefits

"For the past ten years we have tried, like our competitors, to develop a satisfactory search engine that would help our pre-sales people. With catalogues two feet thick describing thousands of ICs, finding the right product or the closest to the customer's needs is not an easy job, even for a well-trained engineer. We tried CBR and in less than a year we had a unique and successful pre-sales tool."

David Kress; Director of Applications Engineering (Analog Devices)

Analog Devices' CBR solution provides significant benefits to their customers. Product information is available 24×7, and improved customer support during product selection increases customer satisfaction both on the Web and via the interactive CD-ROM. Comprehensive and current product knowledge is available to customers through a focused product search. Instead of a time-consuming search and the formulation of complex database queries, customers now simply provide an example of a product with the broad characteristics of their requirements. Users can express their preferences by assigning weights to different product features, and the use of filters can limit the search to certain sets of products.[3]

These partially formulated demands lead to the retrieval of a list of matching products that are sorted according to their usefulness to the customer. Large sets of products can be presented in a meaningful way, and if a precise match cannot be found, at least the best alternatives are shown. In addition, the collection of customer profiles from the Web site provides information on trends, resulting in invaluable feedback for future product development and marketing at Analog.

---

3 Remember in Chapter 2 I described how a nearest neighbor algorithm can use feature weights to assign relative importance to individual features. This is a good example of feature weights being used in practice.

"We see the Internet as offering great opportunities for supporting our customers, and we see that case-based reasoning is in a unique position to improve the support we provide."

Grayson King, Analog Devices

Analog Devices is obtaining significant year-on-year savings, since the cost of producing and shipping 120,000 CD-ROMs and maintaining the Web sales site is substantially less than the paper catalogues they have replaced.

7.6 Conclusion

CBR technology has introduced intelligent sales support to e-commerce applications at Analog Devices. The limitations of standard database techniques were overcome by adding knowledge to the retrieval system. CBR removes the problem of near misses, reduces the need for expert-level knowledge on the customer's side, and by improving the usefulness of the search process, reduces customer frustration.

Despite the success of the Analog Devices system, improvements can be made, in particular through the development of interfaces for interactive adaptation and product configuration. CBR-related techniques for indexing and clustering a case base could be used to help customers refine their queries through a step-by-step analysis of their needs. By analyzing the structure of the case base, a CBR system can suggest which undefined parameters the user should define next in order to find a good solution as quickly as possible. It is also possible to explain to customers the reasons why the retrieved results are suitable for their query. Personalized product configuration is the next challenge for us.

Distributed Sales Support
Web-Based Engineering at Western Air

Ian Watson
AI-CBR
Department of Computer Science
University of Auckland

8.1 Introduction

Western Air is a distributor of HVAC (heating ventilation and air conditioning) systems in Australia with a turnover in 2000 of $40 million (Australian dollars). Based in Fremantle, the company operates mainly in Western Australia, including isolated communities in the Great Sandy, Great Victoria, and Gibson deserts—a geographic area of nearly 2 million square miles. The systems supported range from simple residential HVAC systems to complex installations in new and existing factories and office buildings.

8.2 The Problem

Western Air has a distributed sales force numbering about 100. The majority of staff do not operate from head office but are independent, working from home or a mobile base (typically their car). In fact many sales staff seldom visit Fremantle. They are technically trained, being required to take a four-week training course covering most aspects of the systems they supply. They do not install systems; this work is done by specialist subcontractors.

Simple installations, such as a set of window- or exterior wall–mounted AC box units, can be easily specified and priced by even the most novice salesperson. However, the specification and cost estimation of more complex systems involving roof-mounted AC units, ducting, fans, and sensors require the expertise of a fully qualified HVAC engineer. Western Air about five fully qualified engineers (two of whom are the firm's owners). Until recently, sales staff in the field would gather the prospective customer's requirements using standard form and proprietary software, take measurements of the property, and fax the information to Western Air in Fremantle. A qualified engineer would then specify the HVAC system. Typically the engineer would have to phone the salesperson and ask for additional information. Usually the salesperson would have to make several visits to the customer's building and pass additional information back to the engineer.

The engineer would then specify and cost the installation, and a quote would be prepared and faxed to the salesperson, who would forward the quote to the customer. If necessary, the salesperson was empowered to negotiate on price within set margins. If the customer then decided that perhaps he needed fewer sensors or now only wanted certain zones in the building cooled, the salesperson would have to contact the engineer and repeat the cycle.

This process could take several weeks if the engineers were busy with other work, and during this process the salesperson may be detained "beyond the Black Stump" (Australian slang for "a remote place" such as Kununurra in the far north) or lose the sale to a competitor.

When preparing specifications and quotes, engineers use a variety of specialized software to calculate HVAC loadings and make extensive use of previous installations. In particular, Western Air felt that basing a quote on the price of a previous similar installation gave a more accurate estimation than using prices based on proprietary software, catalogue equipment prices, and standard labor rates. However, they were aware that they were not making use of all their past work. They had nearly 10,000 system installation files, but most engineers only made use of their favorite few dozen. To try to help engineers make use of all the past installations, a database was created to let engineers search for them. The database records contained about thirty to sixty fields describing the key features of each installation and then a list of file names for the full specification. These might be Word documents, Excel files, or AutoCAD files.

Initially the engineers liked the database, and it increased the number of past installations they used as references. However, after the honeymoon ended, they started to complain that it was too hard to query across more than two or three fields at once, and that querying across ten or more fields was virtually impossible. In fact most of them admitted to using the database to laboriously browse through past installations until they found one that looked similar to their requirements.

8.3   The Knowledge Management Solution

Western Air realized they wanted a system that could find similar installations without making the query too complex for the engineers. By chance they employed a new engineer (Dan Gardingen) who had been introduced to CBR while doing a computer science master's degree in the U.K. Web-based CBR applications have been demonstrated for a few years now, and Dan therefore felt that CBR on the Web was suited for this project and contacted AI-CBR for advice.[1]

Western Air decided that merely improving the efficiency of the engineers in Fremantle would not solve the whole problem. Ideally they would like the sales staff to be able to give fast, accurate estimates to prospective customers on the spot. However, they were aware that there was a danger that the less knowledgeable sales staff might give technically incorrect quotes.

The solution they envisaged was to set up a Web site that sales staff could access from anywhere in the country. Through a forms interface, the prospect's requirements could be input and would be passed to a CBR system that would search the library of past installations and retrieve similar installations. Details of the similar installations along with the FTP addresses of associated files would then be available to the sales staff by FTP. The sales staff could then download the files and use these to prepare an initial quote. All this information would be automatically passed back to an engineer to authorize or change if necessary. Once an installation was completed, its details would be added to the library and its associated files placed on the FTP server.

8.3.1 Expected Benefits

Western Air expected the following benefits:

- A reduction in the time taken to turn around sales quotes from an average of five days to two days. It was estimated this might save approximately $250,000 a year.
- An increase in the accuracy of their estimates, allowing them to judge their margins better and be more competitive. If they were able to reliably increase their margins (while keeping their quotes competitive) by 1 percent, it would increase profits by $500,000 a year.

---

1 Contact details for CBR consultants can be found in the Appendix.

8.3.2 The Team

The development team comprised:

- a senior engineer from Western Air (one of the firm's owners) as project champion,
- an engineer from Western Air to act as project manager and subject matter expert,
- a consultant Java/HTML programmer,
- a consultant from AI-CBR to advise on CBR issues, and
- a part-time data entry clerk.

8.3.3 Implementation Plan

The project had the direct involvement of one of the firm's owners, so management commitment was not a problem. It was also decided that creating a partially functional prototype was not sensible since the system would either work or not. However, a carefully controlled and monitored trial was considered essential for two reasons:

- It was still not certain that sales staff could create technically sound first estimates, and therefore a small, carefully monitored trial was essential to avoid losing money.
- There were resource implications because some of the portable PCs being used by sales staff were old 486 Windows 3.1 machines, and few of them had modems or Internet accounts.

A fixed (nonnegotiable) budget of $50,000 was given to the project, and it was decided that six months would be given for development and trial of the system. The project started in October 1997 and the trial was planned for March 1998.

It was decided initially to deal with moderately complex residential HVAC systems because this would provide a reasonable test of the system without undue risk. Western Air felt that it was commercially unwise to risk experimentation on high-value commercial contracts.

8.3.4   Hardware and Software

A Windows NT server was purchased to act as both Web and FTP server. The team decided to keep the HVAC information in the original database (MS Access) since this would remove the need to create a new case library. They began an evaluation of commercially available CBR tools with Web facilities, including products by eGain, Empolis, Kaidara, Haley, and MindBox.[2] However, since a simple nearest neighbor retrieval algorithm would almost certainly suffice, implementing their own system was deemed a viable option. Java (Visual Café) was chosen as the implementation language for both the client and server elements of the CBR system. The XML standard (eXtensible Markup Language) was used as the communication language between client- and server-side applets.

The World Wide Web Consortium finalized XML 1.0 in December 1997 as a successor to HTML. HTML provides a fixed and limited tag set, whereas XML authors can define an unlimited number of tags. XML therefore can incorporate commands that can be interpreted by applications and user-defined attribute:value pairs. Thus, XML is a natural communications standard for distributed intelligent systems operating on the Web.

8.3.5   System Architecture

Figure 8.1 shows the system architecture. On the sales staff (client) side, a Java applet is used to gather the customer's requirements and send them as XML to the server. On the server side, another Java applet (a servlet) uses this information to query the Access database to retrieve a set of relevant records. The Java servlet then converts these into XML and sends them to the client-side applet that uses a nearest neighbor algorithm to rank the set of cases.

---

2 Contact details for CBR software vendors are given in the Appendix.

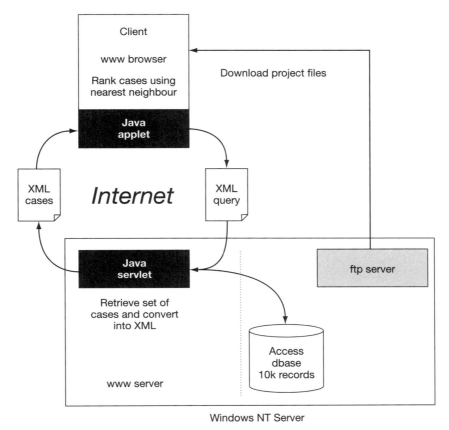

Figure 8.1   System architecture.

8.3.6   Case Representation

Cases are stored permanently within a Microsoft Access database as conventional database records. Each record (case) comprises between thirty to sixty fields used for retrieval and many more used to describe the HVAC installations. In addition, links to other files on the FTP server are included to provide more detailed descriptions.

Once retrieved from the database, the records are ranked by a nearest neighbor algorithm and dynamically converted into XML for presentation to the client browser. XML pages can contain any number of user-defined tags defined in a document type definition (DTD) file. Tags are nested hierarchically from a single root tag that can contain any number of child tags. Any child tag in turn can contain any number of child tags. Each tag contains a begin statement (for example, <Case>) and an end statement (for example, </Case>). This is illustrated in Figure 8.2.

8.3.7 Case Acquisition

Western Air had already put a considerable amount of effort into developing their HVAC installation database, which was used as the case library for our system. Consequently the project was fortunate in not having to acquire cases or preprocess them. However, knowledge engineering was required to create similarity metrics and obtain default weightings for the retrieval algorithm. This was not surprising, as the

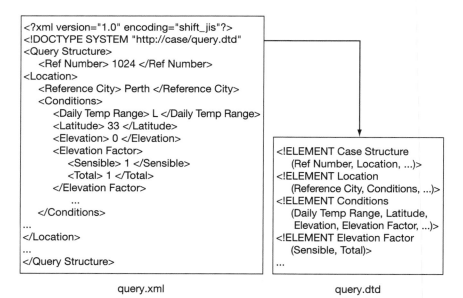

query.xml   query.dtd

Figure 8.2   Sample of the XML case description.

similarity measure is one of the most important knowledge containers of any CBR system.[3]

8.3.8 Case Retrieval

Case retrieval is a two-stage process. In stage one the customer's requirements are relaxed through a process of query relaxation. What this process does is to take the original query and relax certain terms in it to ensure that a useful number of records are retrieved from the database. This is similar to the technique used in a CBR system called SQUAD at NEC in Japan. For example, let us assume that we are trying to retrieve details of properties in or near Perth in the southwest of the state. An SQL query that used "Perth" alone as a search term might be too restrictive. Using a symbol hierarchy, our system knows that Perth is in the southwest of the state, so the query is relaxed to `Where (((Location,ReferenceRegion) = "SW")..))`. This query will include installations from Perth, Fremantle, Rockingham, and surroundings. Similarly, specific elevations or temperatures can be relaxed to ranges (for example, "Between 60 And 70"). Figure 8.3 shows an example of a relaxed query.

Determining exactly how the query could be relaxed involved knowledge engineering and, for example, involved creating symbol hierarchies for location, building types, and usage. The Java servlet queries the database to retrieve a set of broadly similar records. If too few records are retrieved (five is considered to be enough), the query is relaxed further. If too many records are retrieved (more than twenty), the query is made firmer to reduce the number. Once a sufficient set of records has been retrieved, they are converted into XML and sent to the client-side applet.

---

3 Processor Michael Richter of the University of Kaiserslautern in Germany has postulated that a CBR system contains knowledge in the following "containers": the case representation, the case indexes, the similarity metrics, the retrieval algorithm, and the adaptation methods.

```
SELECT Location.ReferenceRegion, Location.DailyTempRange, Location.Lattitude,
Location.Elevation, Location.ElevationFactorS, Location.ElevationFactorT,
Location.DryBulbTempWin, Location.DryBulbTempSum, Location.WetBulbTemp,
...
FROM Location
WHERE (((Location.ReferenceRegion)="SW") AND ((Location.Elevation) Between 0
And 100) AND ((Location.DryBulbTempWin) Between 50 And 60) AND
((Location.DryBulbTempSum) Between 60 And 70))
...
```

Figure 8.3   Example of an SQL query that has been relaxed.

In the second stage the small set of retrieved records are compared by the client-side applet with the original query, and similarity is calculated using a simple nearest neighbor algorithm.

Western Air expressed some surprise at the necessity for this second step and did not see the need for calculating a similarity score. Initially they felt that it would be sufficient to show only the small set of retrieved records. However, during the trials the sales staff found that the similarity score was useful. Moreover, once they understood the principle, they could override the default feature weightings if they wished, which they also found useful. Changing the weightings let them reflect either the customer's preferences or their own experience.

8.3.9 Case Retention

Once an HVAC installation is completed, its details are added to the Access database and its associated files placed on the FTP server. Having a database management system for the case repository has proved very helpful since it makes it easier to generate management reports and ensure data integrity. It would be almost impossible to maintain a collection of 10,000 cases without a DBMS.

8.3.10   Interface Design

The interface to the system is a standard Java-enabled Web browser (Netscape or Internet Explorer). The forms within the Java applet were designed to look as similar to the original forms, HVAC specification tools, and reports that the sales staff were already familiar with. Microsoft FrontPage 98 was the primary tool used to create the Web site.

8.3.11   Testing

Two weeks before trial, five test scenarios were created by the project's champion. These were representative of the range of more complex residential installations the system would be expected to handle. The project's champion (an experienced HVAC engineer) knew what the correct answers should be. These were given to the five sales staff who would initially use the system, and they were asked to test the system. Out of the twenty-five tests (5×5), twenty-two were correct. Although the remaining three were not specified as expected, they were felt to be technically acceptable solutions.

8.3.12   Rollout

The system was rolled out for trial to the five sales staff in March 1998. At first the project's champion monitored all the projects that were being processed by the system. As his confidence grew in the system this was reduced to a weekly review.

Acceptance of the system from the five sales staff was very good once they understood what it was doing. At first they expected it to be calculating HVAC loads, as the software they had previously used had done. Once they understood that it was interrogating Western Air's database of HVAC installations, they understood how it could be used to provide them with much more than just HVAC loads. During the month's trial the system dealt with sixty-three installations, all of which were felt to be technically sound. The sales staff had not had to use the expertise of the HVAC engineers at all for this work, although the engineers checked the final specifications.

8.4 System Demonstration

The following screen captures show how the system looks and feels. The first screen (Figure 8.4) shows part of the capture of the customer's requirements. Figure 8.5 shows a retrieved case (judged 95 percent similar) detailing the specification and performance of the HVAC equipment. Figure 8.6 shows specification for ducting, and Figure 8.7

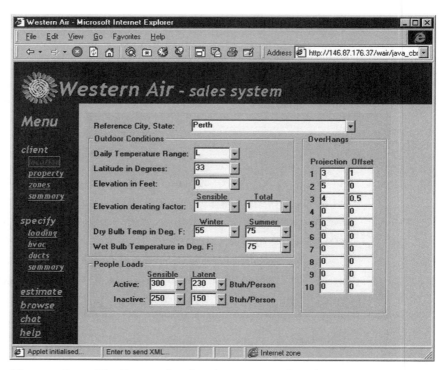

Figure 8.4   The Java applet showing property location.

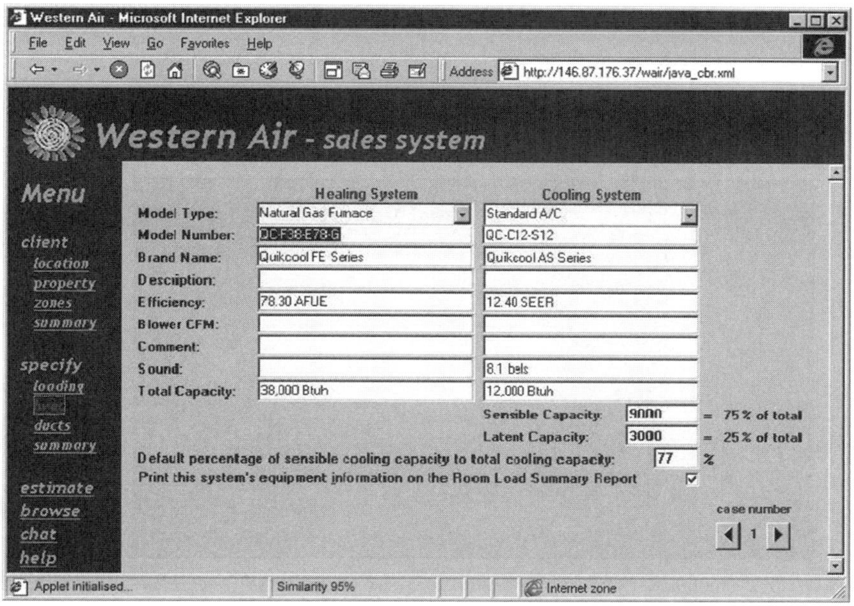

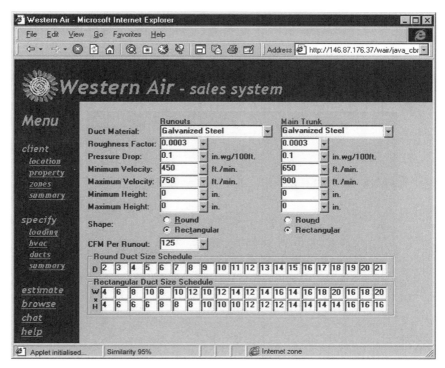

Figure 8.5 Java applet showing HVAC details for a retrieved case.

Figure 8.6 Java applet showing specifications of AC ducting.

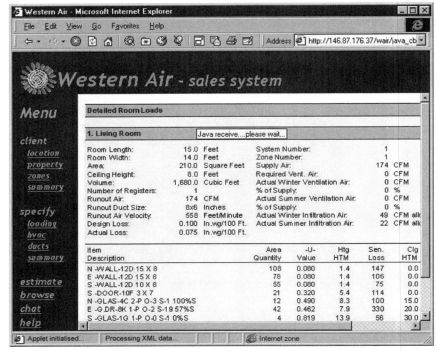

Figure 8.7   Java applet showing summary of HVAC room loading.

shows a summary screen detailing HVAC loads in the customer's living room.

8.5 Benefits

The sixty-three installation projects handled by the five sales staff alone during the trial month resulted in a considerable saving in engineers' time, allowing them more time to deal with complex high-value commercial HVAC contracts. It was estimated that margins had been increased by nearly 2 percent while still remaining competitive. Based on this, Western Air has invested $200,000 in Pentium notebook PCs for its sales staff. The system was rolled out to the entire sales staff in May 1998. In the following financial year Western Air attributed an increase in profits of almost $900,000 to the use of the system—a more than reasonable return on their investment.

One of the firm's senior engineers commented, "Since this system went live I've had much more time to spend on my own contracts. I used to hate going into the office because I always had a string of problems to handle from the mob out in the field. Now I feel I have the time to really help when I do get a problem to deal with."

A member of the sales staff said, "This is just great. It used to be really frustrating waiting for them back in Fremantle to deal with our problems. I always had to give 'em aggro, and when we did finally get an answer the bloody customer changed his mind. Then they whinge because we can't give them an answer on the spot. Now I can even use their phone and get good answers real quick. It really impresses them!"

8.6   Maintenance

In May 1998, the case base contained approximately 10,000 records. These were all relatively recent HVAC installations dating back no more than five years. Projects were not consistently stored in a digital format until the mid-1990s.

The company employs approximately 100 sales engineers, each of whom deal with an average of five quotations a week. (This average is a little misleading since project size and complexity vary greatly, from simple residential systems to complex retail and commercial systems.) Engineers work for forty-eight weeks in the year, and so the company generates about 24,000 specifications and quotations a year. The company expects to win about 25 percent of the tenders (6,000 installations). Of these, from 10 percent to 20 percent will not proceed because customers will change their minds for some reason. Thus, the company expects to perform about 5,000 HVAC installations per year. Actual figures are shown in Table 8.1.

Table 8.1 Number of HVAC installations by year.

Year	No. installations
1998 (May–Dec)	2633
1999 (Jan–Dec)	5174
2000 (Jan–May)	1984
total =	9791

All successfully completed installations were initially retained in the case base. The number of installations is therefore directly equivalent to the number of new cases retained by the system. Thus, the case base practically doubled in two years (from 10,000 to 19,791 cases). This considerable growth raised concerns about the utility problem with respect to case retrieval and suggested that a case deletion technique would be required to control the case base growth.[4]

The following sections describe how two case base maintenance (CBM) issues were dealt with, namely, functionally redundant cases and obsolete cases.

8.6.1 Functionally Redundant Cases

Many HVAC installations are very similar, even identical. For example, within a new housing development several identical house designs may be repeated. Moreover, a developer frequently builds identical

---

4 The "utility problem" refers to the usefulness of individual cases in the memory. In a small case base, individual cases have a high utility (deleting a case would reduce the case base's effectiveness). But as the number of cases increases, cases can start to overlap in terms of functionality; thus, deleting any individual case may not impair the memory's effectiveness. However, as the size of the case base increases, performance, in terms of retrieval speed, may start to be adversely affected. This then is the utility problem—balancing the usefulness of individual cases against the overall performance of the case base.

properties in different locations. Thus, the case base contains many functionally identical cases with different location and client details.

The system has a two-stage retrieval process. In the first server-side process a set of similar cases (approximately twenty) is retrieved from the database and sent to the client-side applet. Clearly, there is no point in sending twenty identical cases where one would suffice.

Several solutions to this problem were considered:

1. Send only one case to the client when all cases in the retrieved set are identical. This was rejected because the servlet does not know that the cases have the same similarity measure. The SQL query retrieves a set that matches within defined limits; the production of a numeric similarity metric is done by the client-side applet. Moreover, even if this were possible, it is undesirable because the sales engineers want to be presented with a set of alternatives from which they choose and create a solution. They do not want to be given a single solution.

2. Change the retrieval algorithm on the server side so that it could measure similarity, reject identical redundant cases, and construct a useful set of alternatives to send to the client applet. This was rejected because it would have meant completely changing the server-side algorithm, which was felt to be working fine. Moreover, it didn't confront the problem of the presence of functionally redundant cases in the case base.

3. Examine the case base, and identify and remove functionally redundant cases.

Option 3 was chosen as being the sensible solution. There were three alternative solutions:

1. *Automatic.* An algorithm would be designed to analyze the case base and automatically identify and remove redundant cases. This algorithm could be run periodically (perhaps weekly) to remove redundancy.

2. *Manual.* Someone would periodically examine the case base, and identify and remove redundant records.
3. *Semiautomatic.* An algorithm would analyze the case base and automatically identify sets or clusters of similar cases, flag these, and a person would select one case from the set to represent it; the others would be archived.

Solution 2 was rejected because the task would be difficult and tedious to perform manually. Solution 3 was chosen, at least initially, since its success or failure would help determine whether solution 1 was achievable.

Redundancy Algorithm Design

Each record in the database contains a field to reference installations that were part of a larger development, such as a housing, apartment, or retail development. These units within a large development were likely to be similar or even identical. However, this could not be guaranteed since a proportion of multiple unit developments are made up of unique units. (This is often used as a selling feature.) Moreover this reference does not identify commonly repeating standard designs used by many developers in many locations. Consequently, using an SQL query simply to identify all units within multi-unit development would not solve the problem.

An algorithm had to be developed to inspect the case base and identify all identical cases. The algorithm takes each case in turn and compares it to every case in the case base. Cases that are identical (or exceed a predefined similarity threshold) are added to the case's similarity set and flagged for removal.

It was recognized that comparing each case to every other case is not a computationally efficient solution. However, since the algorithm need only be run periodically and can be run offline overnight or on the weekend, this is unlikely to cause problems in the foreseeable future. Processing time is much cheaper to the company than consultancy time.

Once the similarity sets were identified, the system maintainer could examine each set in turn, choose a single case to represent the set, and set the status flag of the other members to archive.

Redundancy Algorithm Results

The RSI algorithm was run over the case base of 19,791 cases. The similarity threshold was set to 1.0 (identical). A total of 3,587 redundant cases were identified in 77 sets, or 18.1 percent of the cases. This significant percentage was not surprising since if redundant cases were not sufficiently common to be a problem, they would not have been noticed by users.

Since cases could be very similar, though not identical, and still be functionally redundant (that is, there are no significant differences in the HVAC specifications), the similarity threshold was reduced to 0.95 (95 percent similarity). The RSI algorithm now identified 5,427 redundant cases (27.4 percent of the case base).

Selecting a Set Representative

Once the similarity sets were identified, the next task was to examine each set and select a single case to represent it. The remaining cases in the set would have their status flag set to archive and thus be ignored in future case base retrievals. Three strategies were considered:

1. manually select the representative,
2. randomly select the representative,
3. select the median case—that is, the case with the greatest similarity to all cases in the set.

Solution 1, although originally planned to be used, was rejected because the engineer selected to perform the task said that he found it difficult to decide and admitted to randomly selecting a "likely looking candidate"—in effect, little different from solution 2. A simple algorithm was written to select the median cases from each similarity set.

The algorithm creates a list containing the representative case from each similarity set (the case with the highest total similarity to other cases in its set). In the event of several cases having an equal highest total similarity, the first case is selected. These cases are retained, while all other cases in the similarity sets have their status flags set to archive.

The application of this algorithm reduced the case base by 5,329 cases (5,427 cases less one representative from 98 similarity sets). The new case base contained 14,462 cases, which still represents a significant increase in case base size from its original size.

8.6.2 Functionally Obsolete Cases

The second CBM issue related to case obsolescence. Over time HVAC equipment is withdrawn and replaced, and working practices change. Cases referring to installations using obsolete products or techniques need to be deleted from the case base to prevent inexperienced engineers from including them in new specifications and quotes. The company releases weekly technical memoranda by email and specific working practice guidelines that are updated quarterly. Moreover, sales engineers receive training twice a year to ensure that they are up-to-date with current products and practice.

Some CBR systems retain details of obsolete cases since these may provide useful analogies for problem solving in the future. It is not uncommon for troubleshooting or diagnostic case bases to retain cases referring to problems with obsolete equipment because similar problems may occur in future with new equipment. However, management decided that installations using obsolete equipment need not be retained for problem solving.

It is a relatively easy administrative job to search the database to identify records that refer to obsolete equipment, and flag those records as archive so they are not included in the case base retrieval process. This is done each time there is a significant product change. However, changes also need to be made to the symbol hierarchies used by the SQL query relaxation technique. This was not anticipated during the design of the system. Editing the symbol hierarchies to remove obsolete items of equipment or entire classes of equipment is not simple. They are stored as tables within the database, and a good knowledge of the table structure and relations between them is required to ensure that the hierarchy is not corrupted.

It is not clear that this can be done automatically or even semiautomatically. A graphical hierarchy editor would greatly help the editing task and make it more feasible for a domain expert rather than a programmer to do the maintenance. This has been suggested to the company but is currently beyond their budget for the system.

Finally, it still remains unclear how to identify records where obsolete working practices were used since these are not explicitly referred to in the record structure but remain hidden in the supporting files on the FTP server (see Figure 8.1), or are not even recorded at all. Working practices were not considered important during the design of either the database or the CBR system, and this is an ongoing issue that has yet to be resolved.

8.7   Conclusion

This case study has shown how a distributed knowledge management system using CBR can be created on the Web in a relatively short time. Implementing the system for Web delivery made the system much more viable. Just a few years ago we would have had to install the entire system (including the database of 10,000 records) on each salesperson's PC. We would then have had to regularly send them updates to the database. This would have significantly increased the operational costs of the system. Thus the Web is an ideal medium for delivering intelligent support of all types.

The project was most certainly helped by having a ready-made case library, although some knowledge engineering work was still required in determining valid ways of relaxing the SQL queries and creating similarity metrics. At first we thought we could just link to the Access database and do all the work in Access using macros. But the Java applets were probably easier to create, and XML is a useful communications protocol enabling large packets of formatted information to be exchanged thereby reducing network traffic.

Everyone at Western Air is very impressed with the system, and after the successful trial, they had a strong business case to obtain the necessary investment to upgrade all the sales staff computers. Feedback on the first two years of use is positive, and they are now thinking about how they can use the Web to support other activities.

It can be argued that the maintenance issues—namely, the redundancy problems encountered—were due to (or exacerbated by) the design of the system and the two-stage retrieval process in particular. Although the utility problem was not observed (retrieval performance did not suffer), with a case base doubling in size over two years it would have been unwise to ignore the utility problem in the long term.

With the benefit of hindsight, the design should be changed to examine each new case before it is added to the system and only retain it if it is significantly different from other cases already in the case base (that is, the case is useful).[5] This would not only be a simpler algorithm to apply than the maintenance algorithms that were implemented, but it would also completely remove redundancy in the future.

---

5 This method is used by the system described in the General Electric case study in Chapter 4.

Personalizing Information Services

Intelligent Digital TV at ChangingWorlds

Barry Smyth and Paul Cotter

ChangingWorlds

9.1 Introduction

Paul Cotter and Dr. Barry Smyth founded ChangingWorlds in 1999. Headquartered in Dublin, the company has evolved from an innovative startup to a serious player in the market for advanced technologies in the mobile and digital TV domains. ChangingWorlds delivers state-of-the-art personalization technologies in order to transform online content and services into revenues by targeting the right users with the right information and services at the right time, every time. The ChangingWorlds personalization technology has achieved this for a number of the largest corporations in Europe by transforming their existing online business into a fully personalized service, capable of meeting the unique needs of individual customers. This has resulted in increased usage and loyalty, while actively reducing churn, by delivering a more cost-effective and intuitive service for end users. With a strategic focus on the mobile and digital TV markets, the company develops and designs applications specifically for these markets.

In this case study we focus on an emerging information overload problem associated with the digital TV domain—the problem of locating relevant television information as we move toward hundreds and thousands of available TV channels. We argue that such developments will signal an end to the traditional TV guides, and that the only effective solution is the automatic personalization of programming content. We describe the PTV system, a personalized electronic program guide (EPG), operating over the Internet, that automatically learns about the television viewing habits of individual users in order to present these users with daily television guides that are personalized to their individual preferences. We also outline how the PTV system has been recently adapted for a variety of modes of Internet access, including WAP, PDA, and set-top boxes (STBs).

9.2 The Problem

The information overload problem is synonymous with the Internet—it is increasingly difficult for users to locate the right information at the right time. And, if anything, this problem is exacerbated by the new generation of wireless and handheld Internet devices such as WAP-enabled mobile phones and personal digital assistants (PDAs). If our desktop PCs have opened a doorway to the Internet, then the limitations of the current generation of mobile devices (reduced screen size, memory, and bandwidth) can offer only keyhole access to Internet content. Personalization methods may hold the key to solving the information overload problem by customizing the delivery and presentation of relevant information for individual users.

With the arrival of new cable and satellite television services, and the next generation of digital TV systems, we will soon be faced with an unprecedented level of program choice (upwards of 200 channels and 4,000 programs per day over the next few years). Navigating through this space represents a new variation on the information overload theme, and it will become increasingly difficult to find out what relevant programs are showing on a given day.

Of course the digital TV vendors are aware of these issues, and their current solution is the electronic program guide (EPG), providing users with on-screen access to online TV listings. However, simply providing an electronic equivalent of the paper-based TV guide is not a scalable solution to the problem. For example, a typical EPG might cover a sixty minute time slot for five to ten channels in a single screen. This means that even a relatively modest lineup of seventy channels will occupy ten to fifteen screens of information for each sixty-minute slot, or well over 200 screens for each viewing day. (See Figure 9.1.)

The overabundance of channels is not a problem for digital TV users alone. The television broadcasters themselves are faced with the significant problem of how to ensure that viewers will notice their programming content within a sea of alternatives. This is particularly problematic for the smaller broadcasters and could ultimately have a

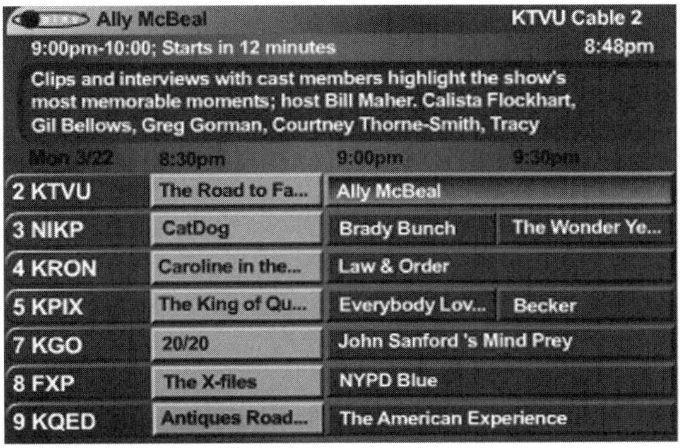

Figure 9.1 Sample EPG listing for seven channels over a one-hour time slot (courtesy of ReplayTV).

negative impact on their ability to attract advertising revenue. In all likelihood, if a solution to this knowledge management problem is not forthcoming, users will probably focus their attention on a small number of larger channels, essentially marginalizing the smaller ones.

Figure 9.2 charts the level of personalization required to support different levels of content in a digital TV setting. The current position is near the origin, with levels of TV content pushing the limits of what traditional nonpersonalized TV guides (hardcopy and online) can hope to usefully handle. The so-called zone of usefulness is wide in this portion of the chart, indicating that many existing EPG solutions are appropriate. However, as the number of TV channels increases (along with the available content), the zone of usefulness narrows rapidly. Traditional, nonpersonalized solutions rapidly move out of this zone, indicating that they are no longer capable of coping with the increased content levels.

We maintain that the only effective solution is to provide a fully personalized EPG that is capable of automatically learning about the viewing

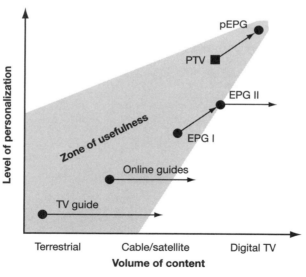

Figure 9.2 Personalization vs. content in the digital TV domain.

needs and preferences of individual users and of alerting these users to the right programs at the right times. If successful, this type of EPG will remove the traditional channel boundaries to offer viewers their own personalized television channel, drawing together relevant programming content from across the full range of available channels no matter how small or big. In this way viewers are guaranteed to receive the right information at the right time, and even the smallest channels will benefit from viewership as long as their program content is relevant to viewers.

9.3   The Knowledge Management Solution

Our solution was designed to provide a scalable personalization technology.[1] (See Figure 9.3.) The system (called ClixSmart) performs two essential tasks:

- It monitors the online activity of users (for a given Web site) and automatically constructs user profiles for these users to capture their domain and behavioral preferences; this task is carried out by the profile manager. The actions of individual users are stored as they select (click), browse, and read content assets, and this information is used to infer interest in specific content assets stored in the content database.
- It uses this learned user profile information to personalize a target Web site by filtering information content for the target user, eliminating irrelevant content items, and highlighting relevant ones.

We used two different content filtering strategies:

- A *content-based* filtering approach seeks to recommend *similar items* to the items that a user has liked in the past.
- In contrast, the *collaborative* recommendation approach seeks to select items for a given user that *similar users* have also liked.

---

1 Because of the very different nature of this problem and solution, it has not been possible to follow the same chapter structure as the preceding case studies.

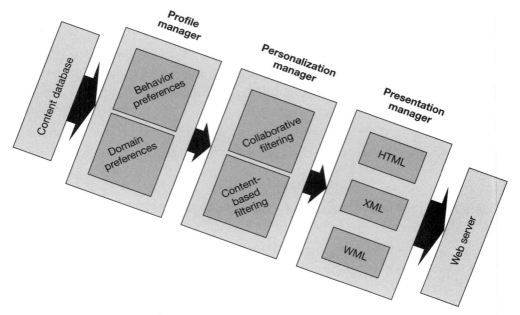

Figure 9.3 System architecture.

9.3.1 Content-Based Filtering

Content-based filtering has its roots in information retrieval and case-based reasoning research. The success of the content-based method relies on an ability to accurately represent recommendable items in terms of a suitable set of content features, and to represent user profile information in terms of a similar feature set. The relevance of a given content item to a specific target user is proportional to the similarity of this item to the user's profile; content-based filtering methods select content items that have a high degree of similarity to the user's profile.

The downside of content-based recommendation methods is that this content description requirement can be problematic and time consuming. In many domains it represents a significant knowledge-engineering problem, and indeed it may not even be possible to develop a suitable content description language in the first place. Content-based methods also suffer from a number of shortcomings in the way that they select items for recommendation. By its very nature, content-based recommendation relies on recommending items that are similar to items that a given user has liked in the past—a user profile effectively delimits a region of the item-space from which all future recommendations will be drawn. Therefore, future recommendations will display limited diversity. This is particularly problematic for new users since their recommendations will be based on the very limited set of items represented in their immature profiles. Items that are relevant to a user, but that bear little or no resemblance to the snapshot of items the user has looked at in the past, will never be recommended in the future.

9.3.2 Collaborative Filtering

Collaborative filtering techniques are a recent alternative to content-based strategies. The basic idea is to move beyond the experience of an individual user profile, and instead to draw on the experiences of a population or community of users. Typically, each target user is associated with a set of nearest neighbor users by comparing the profile information provided by the target user to the profiles of other users. Collaborative filtering techniques look for correlations between users in terms of their ratings assigned to items in a user profile. The nearest neighbor users are those that display the strongest correlation to the target user. These users then act as "recommendation partners" for the target user, and items that occur in their profiles (but not in the target user profile) can be recommended to the target user. In this way items are recommended on the basis of user similarity rather than item similarity.

Collaborative filtering has a number of advantages over content-based methods. First of all, since explicit content representations are not needed, the knowledge-engineering problem associated with content-based methods is relieved. More importantly perhaps, the quality of collaborative filtering typically increases with the size of the user population, and collaborative recommendations benefit from improved diversity when compared to content-based recommendations.

Collaborative filtering does suffer from a number of significant draw-backs. For a start, it is not suitable for recommending new items or one-off content items. This is because collaborative filtering techniques can only recommend items that have already been rated by other users. If a new or one-off item is added to the content database, there can be a significant delay before this item will be considered for recommendation—essentially, only when many users have seen and rated the item will it find its way into enough user profiles to become available for recommendation.

This so-called latency problem is a serious limitation that often renders a pure collaborative recommendation strategy inappropriate for a given application domain. Collaborative recommendation can also prove to be unsatisfactory in dealing with what might be termed an *unusual* user. In short, there is no guarantee that a set of recommendation partners will be available for a given target user, especially if there is insufficient overlap between the target profile and other profiles. If a target profile contains only a small number of ratings or contains ratings for a set of items that nobody else has looked at, then it may not be possible to make a reliable recommendation using the collaborative technique.

Individually, content-based and collaborative personalization methods suffer from a number of significant disadvantages. However, taken together, both techniques complement each other perfectly. For example, content-based filtering can solve the latency problems associated with collaborative filtering. Furthermore, the diversity problem associated with content-based methods is solved by introducing a collaborative component. By integrating both content-based and collaborative filtering strategies, the ClixSmart personalization engine provides a unique and powerful personalization solution.

9.3.3 Implementation Plan

The PTV content database is made up of a schedule database and a program database. The schedule database stores the current channel schedules and is automatically compiled from television station Web sites and bulletin boards. Each schedule item includes a program name, its channel and time information, and a textual episode description. The program database contains information about individual programs and films. Each program record is encoded as a set of features including program name, genre, country of origin, cast, studio, director, writer, and so on. The program database is vital for the content-based personalization component of PTV.

The main function of PTV is to construct personalized TV guides for each individual user. Each guide contains programs that the user is known to enjoy as well as program recommendations that are relevant to the user given her or his current profile. The key to the success of PTV is its ability to select truly relevant program recommendations by using the content-based and collaborative personalization techniques supported by the ClixSmart engine. In this way PTV benefits from all the advantages of a hybrid recommendation system, including the ability to make high-quality and diverse program recommendations, the ability to cope with new or one-off programs, and the ability to cope with new or unusual users.

An example of a personalized guide produced by PTV is shown in Figure 9.4, which shows four separate listings for three programs, *Friends, Married with Children,* and *Ally McBeal.* This guide has been produced for a user with a strong interest in American sitcoms. The user has previously expressed an interest in programs such as *Friends,* and PTV has further recommended *Married with Children* and *Ally McBeal,* which the user has not encountered before, but which PTV feels are relevant.

Since *Married with Children* and *Ally McBeal* are recommendations from PTV, the user is afforded the opportunity to rate these suggestions by clicking on the grading icons (thumbs-up and thumbs-down icons) beside these programs. Importantly, this type of information allows PTV to learn about a user's specific and general viewing preferences. For example, if *Ally McBeal* is rated positively (small or large thumbs-up), PTV will learn not only that the user is interested in this particular program, but also that the user is interested in a range of similar programs such as other American sitcoms, courtroom dramas, and so on. Moreover, PTV will also learn about more general viewing preferences, such as the fact that the user likes to watch shows on Network 2 that air during prime time.

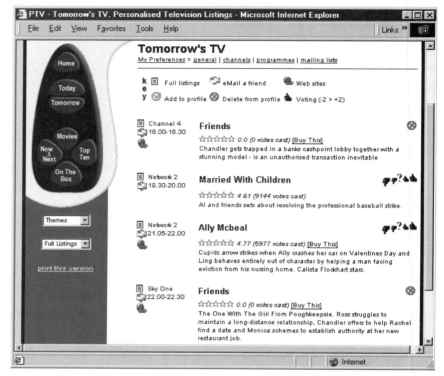

Figure 9.4   Sample PTV personalized TV guide.

The ultimate judgment of a user's interest in a program is whether the user actually watches it, but in the current incarnation of the PTV system there is no way of capturing this information directly by monitoring a user's online behavior. However, ultimately users will be able to access systems like PTV through their television sets, and then it will be possible to recognize whether a user watches a recommended show, thereby doing away with the need to elicit direct feedback.

9.4 System Demonstration

PTV has recently been adapted for a variety of Internet touchpoints including WAP devices, PDAs, and TV set-top boxes, and in this sec-

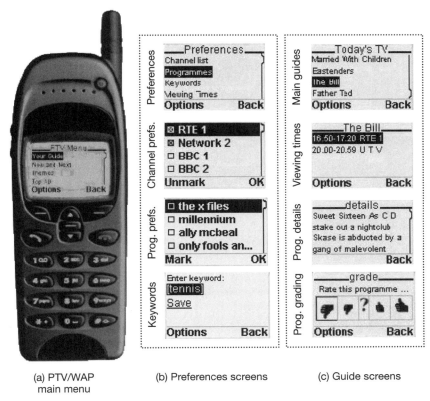

(a) PTV/WAP
main menu

(b) Preferences screens

(c) Guide screens

Figure 9.5 (a) The PTV/WAP main menu; (b) Preferences screens; (c) part of a personalized guide, including viewing times, program description, and grading screens.

tion we provide a brief overview of these new services. Because of the limitations, such as restricted screen space, associated with non-PC modes of Internet access, the importance of personalization takes on a whole new meaning. For example, current WAP devices, such as WAP-enabled mobile phones, offer a screen area that is 1/80th that of a typical PC monitor, and so it is vitally important that valuable screen real estate is not wasted on irrelevant content.

Figures 9.5 and 9.6 show the WAP and PDA versions of the PTV system. Both versions offer the same functionality as the Web-based version of PTV, but are specially customized for the WAP and PDA

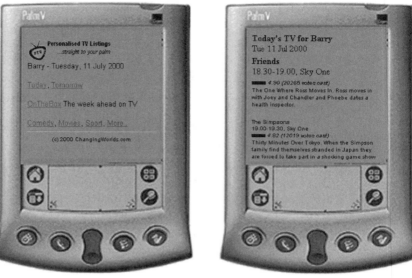

PTV/PDA main menu   PTV/PDA today's TV
(a)   (b)

Figure 9.6   (a) The PTV/PDA main menu and (b) a PTV/PDA personalized guide, including program ratings.

environments. In addition, PTV has been customized to work with a variety of Internet-enabled STBs, including the NetGem STB.

9.5 Benefits

Ultimately the success of the PTV system depends on the quality of its program recommendations and on the appropriateness or relevance of its personalized TV guides.

    To measure the precision of the personalized guides produced by the PTV personalization engine, we carried out a comprehensive user study in the first half of 1999. Regular and new users of the Web-based PTV system were asked to evaluate the system in terms of guide precision, ease of use, and speed of service. The guide precision results are

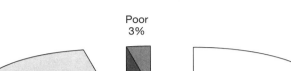

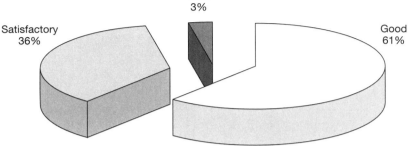

Figure 9.7   Results from the PTV user trial.

of interest here. A total of 310 PTV users were included in the evaluation, and in terms of guide quality (precision), they were asked to rate the appropriateness of their personalized guides. The results, presented in Figure 9.7, were extremely positive. The average personalized guide contained between ten and fifteen programs, and 97 percent of users rated the quality of these guides as satisfactory or good, with only 3 percent of users rating the guides as poor quality.

9.6   Conclusion

Content personalization technologies solve the information overload problem by automatically learning about the information needs of individual users, in order to customize the delivery of the right content to the right user at the right time. The information overload problem extends well beyond the traditional Internet domain, and with the advent of new mobile/wireless and digital TV services, this problem will make its way into all of our lives everyday. PTV is one example of a successful personalized information service, operating in the domain of TV listings, and designed specifically to address the information overload problem in the digital TV space. As a Web service, PTV has attracted over 15,000 users (nearly 5 percent of the Irish Internet user population). Systems like PTV are vital for the success of the digital TV industry in order to equip users with the tools to help them navigate through the maze of television content that digital TV brings. We have also outlined recent developments to adapt the PTV systems for alternative modes of Internet access, including WAP, PDA, and STB touchpoints.

The personalized information services such as PTV also facilitate a whole range of additional services as a side effect of the personalization process. For example, PTV also acts as a personalized entertainment store in the sense that personalized guides contain links to TV-related products. For example, consider someone who is a fan of the TV comedy *Friends*. Her personalized TV guide will not only contain listings for this program, but also links to special merchandise offers available through PTV's retail partners. Thus, a personalized TV listings service adds value by offering one-to-one marketing capabilities.

To date, the ClixSmart technology has been licensed to a number of clients, and a range of personalized systems can be accessed freely on the Internet. Interested readers are encouraged to access the following personalized TV services:

- *www.ptvplus.com.* The main PTV portal site
- *mmm.ptv.ie.* The PTV mobile WAP site
- *www.ireland.com.* The MyTV service
- *www.unison.ie/tv.* STB-based personalized TV listings service

III

Conclusion

10

Lessons Learned

10.1 Introduction

The previous seven case studies have described a variety of successful knowledge management systems, all using case-based reasoning. The implementations and their organizational contexts vary greatly, from large multinational companies such as National Semiconductor and General Electric, to small engineering firms such as Western Air, to Internet startups such as ChangingWorlds. Given the range and variety of knowledge management systems, the purpose of this chapter is to make explicit the lessons learned from the case studies—to draw out common themes to help you understand the issues involved in successfully implementing knowledge management solutions that use case-based reasoning.

I will consider each case study against a variety of features, ranging from the experience levels (with regard to CBR) of those involved in the implementations, to specific details such as whether automatic case revision or adaptation was used. I will also summarize the lessons learned during a decade of the application of CBR to knowledge management.

The following sections present a table summarizing the feature under discussion with respect to each case study, along with an explanation of important issues.

10.2 Prior Experience with CBR

If an organization already has experience in implementing case-based knowledge management systems, successfully or otherwise, it is more likely that subsequent systems will be successful. Table 10.1 shows that over half the organizations had prior experience with CBR. General Electric in particular had considerable experience, having implemented a range of systems, from ones that diagnose faults in diesel locomotives to ones that estimate the value of houses.

It is worth comparing Table 10.1 to Table 10.2, which shows whether external consultants were used to help develop the system. Not surprisingly, there is a correlation between these two. In every case where an organization did not have prior experience in applying CBR, external consultants were used.

Lesson learned: If you do not have prior experience in applying CBR for knowledge management, employ consultants who do.

It is worth noting that in all the examples, once the consultant had trained in-house staff they were able to maintain their system. This means that the organization does not have to reemploy consultants constantly to keep their knowledge management system running. This is also particularly relevant since, as shown in Chapter 1, knowledge management systems are not static (they are not systems that can be bought and used unchanged). Knowledge management systems continually grow and change and therefore require regular planned maintenance.

10.3 Prior Solutions

As Table 10.3 shows, some organizations attempted to solve their knowledge management problem using another technology before they tried a CBR solution. From Chapters 1 and 2, we know that CBR is particularly suitable to knowledge management because the relatively flexible case representations are better suited to representing explicit knowledge as well as tacit and contextual knowledge.

Table 10.1   Did the organization have experience in using CBR?

Organization	Yes	No
National Semiconductor		✓
General Electric	✓	
QPAC (aluminum foundry)	✓	
Deloitte & Touche	✓	
Analog Devices		✓
Western Air		✓
ChangingWorlds	✓	

Table 10.2   Were external consultants used?

Organization	Yes	No
National Semiconductor	✓	
General Electric		✓
QPAC (aluminum foundry)	✓	
Deloitte & Touche		✓
Analog Devices	✓	
Western Air	✓	
ChangingWorlds		✓

Table 10.3   Were previous technological solutions attempted?

Organization	Yes	No
National Semiconductor	✓	
General Electric		✓
QPAC (aluminum foundry)		✓
Deloitte & Touche		✓
Analog Devices		✓
Western Air	✓	
ChangingWorlds	✓	

Lesson learned: CBR can prove successful where database systems or rule-based expert systems have failed.

- National Semiconductor had a database containing fault information, but problems with querying the database and concurrency of the information made the database ineffective. CBR provided more flexible similarity-based querying, and a better management system solved the concurrency issue.
- General Electric replaced a manual process with CBR.
- QPAC replaced a paper-based system.
- Deloitte & Touche used CBR to support an entirely new process for assessing a company's internal control mechanisms.
- Analog replaced paper-based catalogues and data sheets with a CBR system.
- Western Air, like National Semiconductor, had tried to use a conventional database, which failed due to difficulties in querying. Queries were either too general, resulting in too many hits, or too specific, resulting in no hits. The similarity-based retrieval offered by CBR improves on the retrieval of relevant information.
- ChangingWorlds' system replaces electronic program guides (EPGs) with personalized TV guides using CBR and collaborative filtering techniques. ChangingWorlds made a convincing argument in their case study for why EPGs are destined to fail as the number of digital TV channels increases.

10.4 CBR Software and Development Methodology

Three of the case studies used commercially available CBR software,[1] while the other four developed their own bespoke software solutions. (See Table 10.4.) The nearest neighbor algorithm at the core of the re-

---

1 The Appendix provides contact details for CBR software vendors.

Table 10.4   What CBR software was used?

Organization	Tool
National Semiconductor	Kaidara
General Electric	bespoke
QPAC (aluminum foundry)	bespoke
Deloitte & Touche	ReMind
Analog Devices	Kaidara and Empolis
Western Air	bespoke
ChangingWorlds	bespoke

Table 10.5   What development methodology was used?

Organization	Methodology
National Semiconductor	prototyping
General Electric	prototyping
QPAC (aluminum foundry)	prototyping
Deloitte & Touche	prototyping
Analog Devices	prototyping
Western Air	prototyping
ChangingWorlds	prototyping

trieval process of most CBR systems is relatively easy to implement, particularly if optimizing the performance of the retrieval algorithm is unlikely to be a major issue. Thus if programming skills are available, implementing your own solution is certainly feasible. But using one of the increasingly sophisticated CBR tools on the market is worth considering, particularly if you do not have experience in applying CBR.

Lesson learned: Developing your own CBR software is possible, but usually only if you have programming skills and experience with CBR.

As you can see in Table 10.5, all of the developers broadly followed a rapid-prototyping development methodology. This is particularly

Table 10.6 Did the CBR system replace an existing process that was analogous to CBR?		
Organization	**Yes**	**No**
National Semiconductor	✓	
General Electric	✓	
QPAC (aluminum foundry)		✓
Deloitte & Touche		✓
Analog Devices		✓
Western Air	✓	
ChangingWorlds		✓

suitable for the development of experimental or novel systems involving a small development team.[2]

Lesson learned: CBR systems can be successfully implemented using a rapid-prototyping development methodology.

10.5 Existing Process Analogous to CBR

Table 10.6 shows that in three of the case studies, National Semiconductor, General Electric, and Western Air, the new CBR system replaced a process that was analogous to CBR, albeit a manual one. In the General Electric study technicians were manually searching color samples to find a similar match and then using the retrieved color for-

---

2 In recent years a European research consortium has developed a methodology and support tools specifically for the development of CBR systems. More information can be found in the book *Developing Industrial Case-Based Reasoning Applications: The INRECA Methodology,* by Bergmann, R., Breen, S., Göker, M., Manago, M. & Wess, S. Lecture Notes in Artificial Intelligence, LNAI 1612, Springer Verlag.

Table 10.7   Did cases exist to populate the case-base?

Organization	Yes	No
National Semiconductor	✓	
General Electric	✓	
QPAC (aluminum foundry)	✓	
Deloitte & Touche		✓
Analog Devices	✓	
Western Air	✓	
ChangingWorlds		✓

mula as a basis for the new color. Similarly, in the Western Air study engineers were searching records of past HVAC installations to base new quotations and tenders on.

> *Lesson learned: If an existing process is analogous to the CBR-cycle, it is an excellent indicator that it can be successfully implemented using CBR.*

However, in the majority of the case studies, CBR was used where it was not obviously replacing an existing case-based approach. It is particularly useful for improving upon existing database or information retrieval techniques or in a customer support (help desk) situation.

10.6   Acquisition and Processing of Cases

It would seem to be a prerequisite for cases to exist prior to implementing a CBR system. Basically a knowledge management system must have some knowledge to manage. Thus, it is no surprise that past cases did exist in the majority of studies, as shown in Table 10.7. But organizations develop new products and services or have to respond to changes in legislation or markets all the time. When a new service is created, they may decide to implement a knowledge management system from the outset.

In the Deloitte Touche and ChangingWorlds examples, cases were created to populate the respective systems' case bases—in Deloitte Touche's example, through a methodical case acquisition process, and in ChangingWorlds' example, through the online use of the system.

> *Lesson learned: It is useful to have existing cases upon which to build a CBR system, but cases can be acquired through knowledge engineering or by a system during use.*

If cases exist, perhaps as database records, you might assume that they could simply be imported into a case base. As you can see in Table 10.8, the case studies show that this is rarely so. In all but one of the studies (the QPAC foundry system), where cases existed prior to the implementation of the CBR system, they required preprocessing.

> *Lesson learned: Even if cases already exist, perhaps as records in a database, they will usually require preprocessing.*

Typically, even if good database records exist, they will need scrutinizing for incorrectly entered information and omissions. Moreover, because existing records are usually kept for record-keeping purposes,

Table 10.8   Did existing cases require preprocessing before being added to the case base?

Organization	Yes	No
National Semiconductor	✓	
General Electric	✓	
QPAC (aluminum foundry)		✓
Deloitte & Touche	n/a	
Analog Devices	✓	
Western Air	✓	
ChangingWorlds	n/a	

they may not be useful for problem-solving purposes, as important information may be missing.

In addition, databases that exist for record keeping obviously store every record (every customer, every sale, every trouble ticket, etc.), whereas a knowledge management system only needs to keep those cases that impart some valuable knowledge. Such cases are likely to be a subset of the records in the database. Two of the case studies (General Electric and Western Air) described ways of deciding which case to include in the case base. Typically this involves subject matter experts inspecting cases, but the process may be supported by statistical and other analyses.

10.7   Number of Cases and Case Bases

People are always interested in how many cases are in a case base. It is often one of the first questions asked of a CBR developer. You might assume that more is better, but as the case studies show (see Table 10.9), the correct number of cases depends on the knowledge management problem. In certain domains a relatively small number of high-quality cases were used (National Semiconductor, QPAC, and Deloitte Touche). In other situations cases exist to

Table 10.9   How many cases were in the case base?

Organization	# of Cases
National Semiconductor	200+
General Electric	20,000+
QPAC (aluminum foundry)	200 × 4
Deloitte & Touche	200
Analog Devices	n/a
Western Air	19,000
ChangingWorlds	n/a

represent a wide range of problem situations, and consequently the number of cases required is much higher (General Electric and Western Air). Finally, in some knowledge management systems a case exists for every product or customer (Analog and Changing-Worlds), so the number of cases in the case base is not an important metric.

> *Lesson learned: Large case bases are not necessarily better than small case bases, or vice versa. The correct number of cases depends on your knowledge management problem.*

Although most of the case studies created a single case base within their knowledge management system, in some instances it makes sense to create separate case bases. (See Table 10.10.) Separate case bases were created for each of the aluminum foundries using the QPAC system because their faults and processes differed.

> *Lesson learned: Separate case bases may be required if problems and their solutions from one part of a domain are not useful in another part.*

Table 10.10   How many separate case bases were created in your system?

Organization	# of Case Bases
National Semiconductor	1
General Electric	1
QPAC (aluminum foundry)	4
Deloitte & Touche	1
Analog Devices	1
Western Air	1
ChangingWorlds	1

10.8 Case Representation

Chapter 2 discussed case representations. As Table 10.11 shows, the majority of case bases reported here used a flat case representation similar to the record and field representation of a database. Two of the studies used a more complex structural representation. These were used in National Semiconductor's and Analog's systems to model the structural decomposition of the artifacts being supported (integrated circuits, robots, and operational amplifiers). Structural case representations are more complex to create than flat ones but are good for modeling part-of relationships and hierarchies of classes and subclasses of components. Both Kaidara and Empolis produce CBR tools that support structural case representations.

> *Lesson learned: If your knowledge management problem involves supporting physical artifacts that can be decomposed into parts and subparts, or classes and subclasses, of products, a structural case representation may be appropriate.*

Table 10.11 What case representation was used?

Organization	Case Representation
National Semiconductor	structural
General Electric	flat
QPAC (aluminum foundry)	flat
Deloitte & Touche	flat
Analog Devices	structural
Western Air	flat
ChangingWorlds	flat

10.9 Case Retrieval Technique

As you can see in Table 10.12, the majority of the studies here used the nearest neighbor technique to retrieve cases from the case base. Deloitte & Touche used inductive case retrieval techniques as well. These techniques examine the case base and produce a tree structure to index the cases.[3] The final case study, by ChangingWorlds, showed how CBR could be used with a completely different technique—namely, collaborative filtering—to create a hybrid system. CBR has been used in many hybrid systems alongside a wide variety of computational techniques.

> *Lesson learned: Nearest neighbor is a simple and robust retrieval technique that can be used with other technologies if necessary.*

10.10 Case Revision

Case revision or adaptation is an important process within the CBR-cycle. However, as mentioned in Chapter 2, the revision process is usually performed by people using the retrieved cases as a guide or basis upon which to work. As Table 10.13 shows, the studies here support this. Only General Electric's system performed automated, or computerized, case adaptation. They were able to automate the revision process because the knowledge required to do so could be formalized.

> *Lesson learned: Case revision or adaptation need not be automated. Indeed, there are benefits to keeping people in the loop.*

---

3 Inductive retrieval is described in my previous book: *Applying Case-Based Reasoning: Techniques for Enterprise Systems,* Morgan Kaufmann, 1997.

Table 10.12   What case retrieval technique was used?

Organization	Retrieval Technique
National Semiconductor	nearest neighbor
General Electric	nearest neighbor
QPAC (aluminum foundry)	nearest neighbor
Deloitte & Touche	nearest neighbor and induction
Analog Devices	nearest neighbor
Western Air	nearest neighbor
ChangingWorlds	nearest neighbor and collaborative filtering

Table 10.13   How were retrieved cases revised or adapted?

Organization	Revision Technique
National Semiconductor	manually
General Electric	automatically
QPAC (aluminum foundry)	manually
Deloitte & Touche	n/a
Analog Devices	n/a
Western Air	manually
ChangingWorlds	n/a

In the words of Christopher Riesbeck, one of the early pioneers of CBR:

> Adaptation techniques are hard to generalise, hard to implement, and quick to break. Furthermore, adaptation is often unnecessary. The originally retrieved case is often as useful to a human as any half-baked adaptation of it.[4]

---

4 Reisbeck, C.K. (1996). "What Next? The Future of Case-Based Reasoning in Post Modern AI." In *Case-Based Reasoning: Experiences, Lessons, & Future Directions*, Leake, D.B. (Ed.), AAAI Press/The MIT Press, p. 388.

Moreover, Mark, Simoudis, and Hinkle, pioneers in the application of CBR, state that in their experience:

> One of our consistent findings was that automated adaptation of cases was not feasible. The required depth of domain understanding consistently forced us into ad hoc approaches that had very limited coverage ... On other hand, we found that users are very willing to participate in the adaptation process.[5]

10.11 Case Review

The CBR-cycle described in Chapter 2 advises that before new cases are retained in the case base they should be reviewed. New cases should not be added to the case base if they, for example, contradict existing cases or perhaps if they repeat cases that are already present. As you can see in Table 10.14, only QPAC did not have any form of review process where either subject matter experts reviewed new cases or an automated review was performed. The most common process was for a periodic meeting (for example, monthly) to take place, where subject matter experts and case-based administrators could review new cases and if necessary examine existing cases as well. Western Air and General Electric show that in certain circumstances techniques can be implemented for automating all or parts of the review process.

The importance of the review process and of planning to maintain the case base should not be underestimated.[6]

Lesson learned: Case bases are rarely allowed to grow without a review process to decide which cases should be added to or deleted from the case base.

---

5 Mark, W., Simoudis, E. & Hinkle, D. (1996). "Case-Based Reasoning: Expectations and Results." In *Case-Based Reasoning: Experiences, Lessons, & Future Directions*, Leake, D.B. (Ed.), AAAI Press/The MIT Press, p. 293.

6 A recent special issue of a scientific journal was devoted entirely to the subject of maintaining case-based reasoning systems: *Computational Intelligence*, Vol. 17 No. 2, May 2001, Blackwell Publishers.

Table 10.14   Were new cases reviewed by managers before being retained?

Organization	Review Process
National Semiconductor	yes
General Electric	no (automatic review)
QPAC (aluminum foundry)	no
Deloitte & Touche	yes
Analog Devices	n/a
Western Air	yes (semiautomatic)
ChangingWorlds	n/a

Table 10.15   Was significant organizational change required?

Organization	Yes	No
National Semiconductor		✓
General Electric	✓	
QPAC (aluminum foundry)		✓
Deloitte & Touche		✓
Analog Devices		✓
Western Air	✓	
ChangingWorlds	n/a	

10.12   Organizational Change

It is common for the majority of knowledge management books to emphasize that successful knowledge management initiatives require organizational change and significant changes to the culture of an organization. As you can see in Table 10.15, the case studies reported here do not support this. Only two, General Electric and Western Air, reported significant organizational change as a result of implementing their systems. It is worth commenting, however, that significant organizational change might not be expected in some of the systems with limited scope.

10.13 Conclusion

A lot of hype has been written about knowledge management. I hope this book has dispelled some of your preconceptions. I have avoided dealing in clichés and have not advised that your road to success is by "empowering knowledge workers through leveraging your knowledge assets." Creating a management culture where knowledge can be shared is important, but since most other knowledge management books deal almost exclusively with this subject, this book has focused on how you can implement specific knowledge management systems.

I believe that this is important because you are likely to have more success in implementing a specific knowledge management system with a limited scope than in changing your entire organization's management culture and ethos.

This book has shown through seven case studies that case-based reasoning is an established and mature knowledge management methodology, well suited to the needs of organizational knowledge management. Chapter 1 showed that knowledge must be acquired, analyzed, preserved, and reused. The CBR-cycle, described in detail in Chapter 2, maps to these fundamental requirements almost exactly. Thus CBR provides a way of storing knowledge in a case base, retrieving it by similarity matching, reusing it, revising it, reviewing, and retaining it. Not all of these processes need to be automated. Indeed in some systems only the case base and the retrieval process are computerized.[7]

---

7 Some academics refer to these systems as case-based *retrieval* systems rather than case-based reasoners.

Case-based reasoning is not the only technique that knowledge management systems can use. However, if you decide to use document management, information retrieval, or knowledge-based systems, you'll still come up against the fundamental requirements of having to store, retrieve, reuse, revise, review, and retain knowledge. I would argue that CBR is the only knowledge management solution that provides a methodology for dealing with each of these in an explicit, controlled, and managed way. Regardless of the technology you use to implement your knowledge management system, you will find that a major intangible benefit of a knowledge management initiative is a better understanding of your organization's processes.

Whatever your business sector or organization, I'm sure you can now find several places where a knowledge management system using CBR could be successfully applied. I'm also sure that if you decide to implement a system, you'll have a lot of specific questions. Feel free to contact me, the authors of the individual case studies, and the CBR software vendors and consultants listed in the Appendix. Everyone involved in CBR is enthusiastic about it and committed to its success.

The message I want to leave you with has not changed from my previous book on applying CBR. The fundamental power and success of CBR is its simplicity. CBR is easy to understand because it is how we've always solved problems. It is easy to implement because the techniques are computationally straightforward. Therefore, if you are planning to build a CBR system, please, keep it simple.

Appendix: Resources

Case Study Author Contact Details

The following is contact information for the case study authors in this book. Please feel free to contact them with questions and comments, or to find out more information.

Arthur Hamilton and Blaise Gomes
National Semiconductor
2880 Scott Boulevard
Santa Clara, CA 95050-2554
USA
Art.Hamilton@nsc.com
Blaise.Gomes@nsc.com

William Cheetham and John Graf
General Electric Company
Bldg. K1, Room 5C21A
One Research Circle
Niskayuna, NY 12309
USA
cheetham@crd.ge.com
graf@crd.ge.com

Chris Price
Centre for Intelligent Systems
University of Wales
Aberystwyth
Ceredigion, SY23 3DB
Wales, UK
cjp@aber.ac.uk

Olivier Curet
Deloitte Touche Tohmatsu
127 Public Square, Suite 2500
Cleveland, OH 44114-1303
USA
ocuret@deloitte.com

Sean Breen
Interactive Multimedia Systems
Clara House
Glenageary Park Co. Dublin
Ireland
sbreen@imsgrp.com

Michel Manago
Kaidara International
15 rue Soufflot, 75005
Paris, France
mmanago@kaidara.com

Stefan Wess and Wolfgange Wilke
Empolis Knowledge
Management GmbH
Sauerwiesen 2
67661 Kaiserlautern
Germany
Stefan.Wess@empolis.com

Ian Watson
AI-CBR
Department of Computer Science
University of Auckland
Auckland, New Zealand
ian@ai-cbr.org

Barry Smyth and Paul Cotter
ChangingWorlds
Trintech Building
South County Business Park
Leopardstown
Dublin 18
Ireland
barry.smyth@changingworlds.com
paul.cotter@changingworlds.com

Case-Based Reasoning Software Vendors

The following is a list of companies that develop, retail, and support CBR software tools. They are organized alphabetically by company name. Several companies have offices in more than one locality, but only the head office address is given. Please visit their Web sites to find out more information.[1]

CaseBank Technologies, Inc.
Tel: +1-905-792-0618
http://www.casebank.com
spotlight@casebank.com

eGain Communications Corp.
714 East Evelyn Avenue
Sunnyvale, CA 94086
USA
Tel: +1-888-60-eGain
http://www.egain.com
info@egain.com

empolis GmbH
An der Autobahn 2
33311 Gütersloh
Germany
Tel.: +49-0-5241-80-40-233
http://www.empolis.com
info@empolis.com

The Haley Enterprise
1108 Ohio River Blvd.
Sewickley, PA 15143 USA
Tel: 1-412-741-6420
http://www.haley.com
info@haley.com

Inductive Solutions, Inc.
380 Rector Place
Suite 4A, New York,
NY 10280
USA
Tel: +1-212-945-0630
http://www.inductive.com
roy@inductive.com

---

1 Visit the AI-CBR website (www.ai-cbr.org) for a current list of CBR software vendors and consultants.

Intellix
H.C. Ørsteds Vej 4, 1. sal
1879 Frederiksberg C
Denmark
Tel: +45-7023-3700
http://www.intellix.com
info@intellix.com

Kaidara International
15 rue Soufflot
75005 Paris
France
Tel: +33-0-1-56-22-00
http://www.kaidara.com
info@kaidara.com

MindBox
300 Drake's Landing, Suite 155
Greenbrae, CA 94904
USA
877-650-MIND (Toll free)
http://www.mindbox.com
info@MindBox.com

Stottler Henke Associates Inc.
1660 S. Amphlett Blvd.
Suite 350
San Mateo, CA 94402
USA
Tel: +1-650-655-7242
http://www.shai.com
Stottler@shai.com

Case-Based Reasoning Consultants and Value Added Resellers

The following is a list of companies, organizations, and individuals that provide consultancy services with expertise in CBR. Please visit their Web sites to find out more information.

AI-CBR
Dept. of Computer Science
University of Auckland
Auckland 1
New Zealand
Tel: +64-0-9-373-7599
http://www.ai-cbr.org
ian@ai-cbr.org

BSR Consulting
Wirtstrasse 38
D-81539
Munich
Germany
Tel: +49-89-69-79-82-6
http://www.bsr-consulting.de
info@bsr-consulting.de

B.U. eLearning Competence Center—
   Enabling Technologies
Sede di Roma—via del Maggiolino
163 CAP 00155 Roma
Italia
Tel: +39-6-22133661
www.italdata.it
domenico.grande@sbsitalia.it

Cap Gemini Ernst & Young
   Nederland B.V.
Daltonlaan 100-700
3584 BK Utrecht
Tel: +31-0-30-689-33-94
http://www.nl.cgey.com
info@cgey.nl

Ashok K. Goel
Associate Professor of Computer
   and Cognitive Science
College of Computing
Georgia Institute of Technology
Atlanta, GA 30332-0280
USA
Tel: +1-404-894-4994
http://www.cc.gatech.edu/ai/faculty/goel/
goel@cc.gatech.edu

Intelligent Software Components
C/ Alcalde Barnils 64-68 Edificio Testa
08190 Sant Cugat del Vallès
Barcelona
Spain
Tel: +34-93-56772-72
http://www.isoco.com
ggorriz@isoco.com

Interactive Multimedia Systems
Clara House
Glenageary Park
Co Dublin
Ireland
Tel: +353-1-2840555
http://www.imsgrp.com/imm/
ims_info@imsgrp.com

IPNlis—Laboratorio de Informatica
   e Sistemas
Instituto Pedro Nunes
R. Pedro Nunes
3030 Coimbra
Portugal
Tel: +351-239-700-900
http://www.ipn.pt
amilcar@ipn.pt

IVF Industrial Research
  and Development Co.
Argongatan 30
SE-431 53 Mölndal
Sweden
Tel: +46-31-706-6155
http://www.ivf.se
rafael.amen@ivf.se

Lean Suan Ong
Senior Consultant/Lecturer
Institute of Systems Science
National University of Singapore
25 Heng Mui Keng Terrace
Singapore 119615
Tel: 65-6874-6145
leansuan@iss.nus.edu.sg

MUR ID SYSTEM
Joakima Rakovca 14 b
52 470 Umag
Croatia
Tel: +385-52-741-867
zlatan.mur@pu.tel.hr

Pecoma
Van Swietenlaan 23
9728 NX Groningen
The Netherlands
Tel: +31-50-5201888
http://www.pecoma.nl
knowledge@pecoma.nl

Stottler Henke Associates Inc.
1660 S. Amphlett Blvd.
Suite 350
San Mateo, CA 94402
USA
Tel: +1-650-655-7242
http://www.shai.com
stottler@shai.com

Mr Zhaohao Sun
School of Information Technology
Bond University
Gold Coast
Queensland 4229
Australia
Tel. +61-07-5595-3369
zsun@bond.edu.au

Technomathematics Research
  Foundation
204/17 KH, New Shahupuri
Kolhapur 416001
India
Tel: +91-231-654522
http://education.vsnl.com/tmrf
tmrf@pn3.vsnl.net.in

Index

X